First Edition

P9-CAM-728

triumphlearning™
# Common Core Coach
## English Language Arts 6

**Common Core Coach, English Language Arts, First Edition, Grade 6**   T105NA   ISBN-13: 978-1-61997-433-3
**Cover Design:** Q2A/Bill Smith   **Cover Illustration:** Carl Wiens

**Triumph Learning®** 136 Madison Avenue, 7th Floor, New York, NY 10016 © 2013 Triumph Learning, LLC. Buckle Down and Coach are imprints of Triumph Learning. All rights reserved. No part of this publication may be reproduced in whole or in part, stored in a retrieval system, or transmitted in any form or by any means, electronic, mechanical, photocopying, recording or otherwise, without written permission from the publisher.

Printed in the United States of America.   10 9 8 7 6 5 4 3 2 1

# Contents

W.6.3.a–e; W.6.4; W.6.5;
W.6.6; W.6.10; SL.6.1.a–d;
L.6.1.a, b; L.6.5.a

RL.6.1; RL.6.2; RL.6.3; RL.6.4;
RL.6.5; RL.6.10; SL.6.1.a–d;
L.6.4.d; L.6.5.a

RI.6.2; RI.6.4; RI.6.10;
SL.6.1.a–d; L.6.4.a–d; L.6.6;
RST.6-8.1; RST.6-8.2; RST.6-8.4;
RST.6-8.5; RST.6-8.6; RST.6-8.7;
RST.6-8.10

W.6.2.a–f; W.6.4; W.6.5;
W.6.6; W.6.7; W.6.8; W.6.10;
SL.6.1.a–d; L.6.2.b; L.6.3.b;
L.6.4.a, c; L.6.6

Common Core
State Standards

RL.6.1; RL.6.2; RL.6.4; RL.6.5;
RL.6.6; RL.6.10; SL.6.1.a–d;
L.6.4.d; L.6.5.a

W.6.2.a–c, f; W.6.4; W.6.5;
W.6.6; W.6.7; W.6.8; W.6.9.a;
W.6.10; SL.6.1.a–d; L.6.1.d;
L.6.3.a; L.6.5.c

RI.6.1; RI.6.2; RI.6.3; RI.6.4;
RI.6.5; RI.6.6; RI.6.8; RI.6.10;
SL.6.1.a–d; L.6.4.d; L.6.5.c;
RH.6-8.6; RH.6-8.8;
RH.6-8.10; RST.6-8.8

W.6.1.a–e; W.6.4; W.6.5;
W.6.6; W.6.10; SL.6.1.a–d;
L.6.1.e; L.6.2.a; L.6.4.b

# Reading Literary Nonfiction

**Look at this** picture of a grizzly bear.

Why would an entertainer include a dangerous bear in his act? Why do you think people would pay to see his shows?

## ESSENTIAL QUESTION

*Why would an author want to tell about people or events from long ago?*

**Consider ▶** What was the relationship between P. T. Barnum and Grizzly Adams?

How were Barnum and Adams alike, and how were they different?

# The GREATEST SHOW on EARTH

**PRIMARY AND SECONDARY SOURCES** A primary source is a document written or created by someone who experienced an event. An autobiography is an author's life story. Other primary sources include letters, interviews, speeches, and diaries.

A secondary source is written by someone who was *not* part of an event. Secondary sources include textbooks, biographies, and articles that discuss or report events based on information in primary sources. How can you determine whether paragraph 1 is a primary or secondary source?

**FIGURATIVE LANGUAGE** The meaning of a figurative expression is not determined by knowing the meaning of each word in it. The phrase *conjures up* means "to make appear magically," but it does not mean that in paragraph 2. It is a figure of speech, a type of figurative language. Other types include simile (which uses *like* or *as*), metaphor, and personification. What is the meaning of *conjures up* in paragraph 2?

1   "There's a sucker born every minute!" Many believe P. T. Barnum exclaimed this during his lifetime. There is no proof that he did, but it's easy to understand why such an exclamation would be attributed to Barnum. It fits with what is known about his life and his interactions with James "Grizzly" Adams.

Thinking of Barnum might make you think of a three-ring circus and The Greatest Show on Earth. Thinking of Grizzly Adams conjures up images of huge, menacing bears. The great entertainers Barnum and Adams were an important part of nineteenth-century American culture.

*Phineas T. Barnum*

In your mind, travel back to the nineteenth century in the United States, a period when the Industrial Revolution allowed Americans more leisure time, when people were looking for entertainment. P. T. Barnum was right there to fill the bill.

Barnum made a sport—and a living—out of hoaxes. He enticed others to pay to see his attractions, some real and some not so real. People came to see trained fleas, parading elephants, and a 161-year-old woman!

5    His star attraction, however, was an African elephant named Jumbo. Some people believe that the word *jumbo* didn't exist before Barnum. In fact, Jumbo was already the elephant's name when Barnum bought the animal for his circus. Barnum kept the name Jumbo and used it to advertise his star attraction. The word *jumbo* became a frequently used word in the English language as a synonym for *enormous*.

**CONTEXT CLUES** Context clues are nearby words and phrases that help you figure out the meaning of an unknown word or phrase. What context clues help you figure out the meaning of the figurative expression *fill the bill* at the end of paragraph 3?

**CONNOTATION AND DENOTATION** A word's denotation is the dictionary meaning of the word. A word can also have a connotation; it can imply a judgment or an emotional meaning. For example, the word *inferno* means "a fire." But *inferno* has the connotation of a huge, uncontrollable, destructive fire. What word in paragraph 5 has the connotation of "something bigger than can be described"?

Jumbo's farewell to London

By the mid-1800s, Barnum was showing attractions at Barnum's American Museum in New York City. There, he and Grizzly Adams met to talk about an entertainment deal.

Adams had earned his nickname, "Grizzly Adams," while hunting and trapping grizzly bears in the mountains in and around California. Adams's "Jumbo" was a grizzly named General Fremont. General Fremont and other bears traveled with Adams to New York.

Barnum wrote about Adams, who would grow to be a close friend, saying Adams was nearly as wild as the beasts he hunted and trapped. The two struck an agreement for Barnum to manage Adams's grizzly bear shows in New York.

Barnum had a huge tent set up for the advertised California Menagerie.[1] The show opened to fanfare in the street. An open wagon followed a marching band. Adams and his grizzlies stood on the wagon, with Adams "riding" on Fremont's back.

10 Adams's show attracted thousands of paying customers. After six weeks, though, a combination of injuries and fever sent Adams to bed. A doctor advised him he would not survive much longer. But Adams said he was strong; he gradually improved.

Adams wanted to take the show on the road, but Barnum advised against it. He thought Adams was too ill to continue performing. Insisting that he was healthy enough to continue, Adams asked for a bonus for completing the road tour. Barnum jokingly offered $500—a fortune at that time— because he never thought Adams would live long enough to complete the road tour. Adams accepted. He also accepted a new hunting suit from Barnum for the shows. Adams said, "Mr. B., I suppose you're going to give me this new hunting-dress."

[1]**menagerie** a collection of wild or unusual animals shown in an exhibition

Retorting in their typical jovial banter, Barnum replied, "Oh no. I got that for your successor, who will exhibit the bears tomorrow; besides, you have no possible use for it."

Adams convinced Barnum to let him keep the suit until he was "done with it." Thinking Adams would be done with it soon, Barnum agreed. But Adams got the last laugh.

Adams made it through the ten weeks of shows on the road, although his health was failing. Barnum paid the bonus. Knowing he would not survive much longer, Adams asked his wife to be certain he would be buried in the hunting suit, and he was. He used it until he was "done with it" and then some. While Adams did not survive, stories of the jovial bond between P. T. Barnum and Grizzly Adams certainly did.

**USE REFERENCE SOURCES**
A reference source, such as a dictionary, thesaurus, or glossary, can help readers understand content. In paragraph 12, the author uses the word *jovial* to describe the relationship between Barnum and Adams. Which resource would be the best for finding the meaning of *jovial*?

**ANALYZE AUTHOR'S TECHNIQUE** Literary nonfiction provides facts and information in a creative way. Often the author includes entertaining examples and stories to engage the reader. Look at paragraph 14. How does the author entertain the reader?

**MAKE INFERENCES** When making an inference, a reader uses facts that are stated to support an understanding or an idea that is not stated. Why did the stories about the bond between Barnum and Adams survive? What information in the selection supports your answer?

## Comprehension Check

Look back in "The Greatest Show on Earth" to note uses of figurative language. Use the graphic organizer to write three sentences from the selection that include this kind of language. In your table, explain the meaning of the figurative language. Then use figurative language in a sentence to describe the relationship between Barnum and Adams.

| Example of Sentence with Figurative Language | Meaning |
| --- | --- |
| A. "There's a sucker born every minute!" | There are many people who are easy to fool. |
| B. | |
| C. | |

**D.** Write a sentence using figurative language that describes the relationship between Barnum and Adams.

_____

_____

_____

_____

# Vocabulary

Use the word map below to help you define and use one of the highlighted vocabulary words from the Share and Learn selection you are about to read or another word you choose.

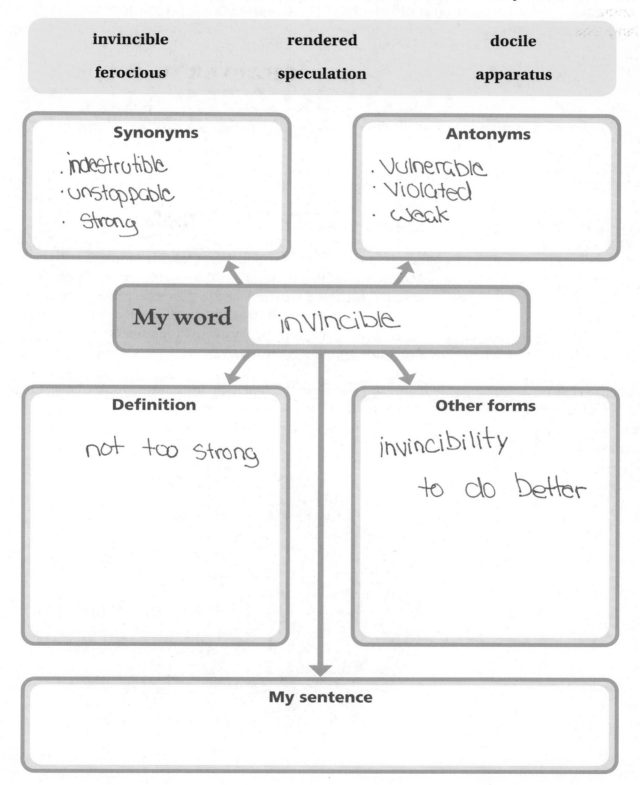

| invincible | rendered | docile |
| ferocious | speculation | apparatus |

**Synonyms**
- indestrutible
- unstoppable
- strong

**Antonyms**
- Vulnerable
- Violated
- Weak

**My word** invincible

**Definition**

not too strong

**Other forms**

invincibility
to do better

**My sentence**

**Consider ▶**  How do "The Greatest Show on Earth" and "Old Grizzly Adams" both tell information in interesting, creative ways?

How does this passage, which was written by Barnum, help you better understand "The Greatest Show on Earth"?

from
## "CHAPTER IV:
# OLD GRIZZLY ADAMS"
in *The Humbugs of the World*
by P. T. Barnum

**CONNOTATION AND DENOTATION**  The word *perils* denotes a danger. What is the connotation of the word *perils*?

_____

_____

_____

**CAUSE AND EFFECT**  What is James Adams's nickname? How did he get that name?

_____

_____

_____

1      James C. Adams, or "Grizzly Adams," as he was generally termed, from the fact of his having captured so many grizzly bears and encountered such fearful perils by his unexampled daring, was an extraordinary character. For many years a hunter and trapper in the Rocky and Sierra Nevada Mountains, he acquired a recklessness which, added to his natural invincible courage, rendered him truly one of the most striking men of the age. He was emphatically what the English call a man of "pluck." In 1860, he arrived in New York with his famous collection of California animals, captured by himself, consisting of twenty or thirty immense grizzly bears, at the head of which stood "Old Sampson"—now in the American Museum—wolves, half a dozen other species of bear, California lions, tigers, buffalo, elk, etc., and "Old Neptune," the great sea-lion from the Pacific.

Old Adams had trained all these monsters so that with him they were as docile as kittens, while many of the most ferocious among them would attack a stranger without hesitation, if he came within their grasp. In fact, the training of these animals was no fool's play, as Old Adams learned to his cost; for the terrific blows which he received from time to time, while teaching them "docility," finally cost him his life.

When Adams and his other wild beasts (for he was nearly as wild as any of them) arrived in New York, he called immediately at the Museum. He was dressed in his hunter's suit of buckskin. . . . In fact, Old Adams was quite as much of a show as his bears. They had come around Cape Horn on the clipper-ship *Golden Fleece*, and a sea-voyage of three and a half months had probably not added much to the beauty or neat appearance of the old bear-hunter.

During our conversation, Grizzly Adams took off his cap, and showed me the top of his head . . . the last blow from the bear called "General Fremont." . . . I remarked that I thought that was a dangerous wound, and might possibly prove fatal.

5 "Yes," replied Adams, "that will fix me out. . . . I'm a used-up man. However, I reckon I may live six months or a year yet."

This was spoken as coolly as if he had been talking about the life of a dog.

**The artist who designed this flag used Grizzly Adams's bear as a model for the drawing.**

**FIGURATIVE LANGUAGE**
Find two instances of figurative language used in paragraph 2. What does each mean?

_____

_____

**COMPARE** How was the behavior of the bears different with Adams and with others? Are wild animals ever completely safe around humans? Explain.

_____

_____

**PRIMARY AND SECONDARY SOURCES**
Is this passage a primary source or a secondary source? How can you tell?

_____

_____

**ANALYZE AUTHOR'S TECHNIQUE** How does the author comment when Adams says he has six months or a year to live? How does this comment change the impact of Adams's response?

_____

_____

**MAKE INFERENCES AND CITE EVIDENCE** Why might the three grizzlies hit or bite Adams occasionally? Cite evidence from the selection that supports your inference.

_____

_____

_____

**CHRONOLOGY** Did this conversation between Barnum and Adams happen before or after the events in the last two paragraphs of "The Greatest Show on Earth"? How can you tell?

_____

_____

_____

**CENTRAL IDEA** What main message does the author give about Adams throughout the selection? Underline examples that convey this message.

_____

_____

_____

The immediate object of "Old Adams" in calling upon me was this. I had purchased one-half interest in his California menagerie from a man who had come by way of the Isthmus from California, and who claimed to own an equal interest with Adams in the show. Adams declared that the man had only advanced him some money, and did not possess the right to sell half of the concern. However, the man held a bill of sale for one-half of the "California Menagerie," and Old Adams finally consented to accept me as an equal partner in the speculation, saying that he guessed I could do the managing part, and he would show up the animals. I obtained a canvas tent, and erecting it on the present site of Wallack's Theatre, Adams there opened his novel California Menagerie.  On the morning of opening, a band of music preceded a procession of animal-cages, down Broadway and up the Bowery; Old Adams dressed in his hunting costume, heading the line, with a platform-wagon on which were placed three immense grizzly bears, two of which he held by chains, while he was mounted on the back of the largest grizzly, which stood in the centre, and was not secured in any manner whatever. This was the bear known as "General Fremont;" and so docile had he become that Adams said he had used him as a packbear to carry his cooking and hunting apparatus through the mountains for six months, and had ridden him hundreds of miles. But apparently docile as were many of these animals, there was not one among them that would not occasionally give even Adams a sly blow or a sly bite when a good chance offered; hence Old Adams was but a wreck of his former self, and expressed pretty nearly the truth when he said:

"Mr. Barnum, I am not the man I was five years ago. Then I felt able to stand the hug of any grizzly living, and was always glad to encounter, single-handed, any sort of an animal that dared present himself. But I have been beaten to a jelly, torn almost limb from limb, and nearly chawed up and spit out by these treacherous grizzly bears. However, I am good for a few months yet. . . . "

## Anchor Standard Discussion Questions

Discuss the following questions with your peer group. Then record your answers in the space provided.

1. The author of the first article describes the bond between P. T. Barnum and Grizzly Adams as "jovial." Based on Barnum's descriptions in the second article, "Old Grizzly Adams," what is another word you could use to describe their friendship? Support your answer with details from the text.

_____

_____

_____

_____

_____

2. How does each article treat the subject of Adams's early death? Support your answer with details from both texts.

_____

_____

_____

_____

_____

## Comprehension Check

1. How does the passage titled "Old Grizzly Adams" differ from "The Greatest Show on Earth"? Support your responses with information from the passages.

_____

_____

_____

2. Suppose Adams had traveled to New York immediately after he captured the grizzly bears, before he spent time training them. What would have been the likely result?

_____

_____

3. Read the following statement made by Adams: "Mr. Barnum, I am not the man I was five years ago. . . . However, I am good for a few months yet. . . ." Why was Adams not the man he had been five years earlier? Based on "The Greatest Show on Earth" and "Old Grizzly Adams," why do you think Adams believed he was "good for a few months yet"?

_____

_____

_____

## Read On Your Own

Read another piece of literary nonfiction, "The Life and Adventures of Alexandre Dumas," independently. Apply what you learned in this lesson and check your understanding.

# Writing Personal Narratives

## ESSENTIAL QUESTION

*What are the characteristics of an effective personal narrative?*

**Doing something** for the first time is an experience that all people have. From visiting relatives you've never seen to meeting your teacher on the first day of school, you have experienced something that is unique to you. There are details about the experience that would give someone else a better picture of what it was like. What did you do? Whom did you see? What did you hear? What did you learn? How did you feel about your experience? People enjoy learning about the experiences of others. One way to share your experiences is to write a personal narrative.

# What's a Personal Narrative?

Everyone has stories to tell about their experiences. An event such as starting at a new school has a story. It has a setting, characters, and a plot. When was your first day? What happened? Who was there? How did you feel? The answers to these questions provide the details for your story.

In a **personal narrative**, you write about an experience in your life. Read the ways to make your personal narrative effective.

### Introduction
Grab the reader's attention and set the scene for your personal story. You may want to briefly introduce the setting—and yourself! Write from the first-person point of view, using words such as *I*, *me*, and *my*.

### Sequence of Events
Tell what happened at the beginning, in the middle, and at the end. Use transition words and phrases, such as *then* and *the next afternoon*, to make the sequence of events clear. Include descriptive details and dialogue to show, rather than tell, what happened and how you felt.

### Conclusion
Share your reflection on your experience. Describe what you learned or how you changed.

Let's look at a personal narrative.

## Analyze a Mentor Text

This is an example of an effective personal narrative by a sixth grader. Read it and then complete the activities in the boxes as a class.

### My First Dance!

⭐ Ugh! I paused nervously in the gym doorway at school. My heart was pounding as I scanned the large crowd several times, looking for my friends. The black dress and patent leather flats that I'd borrowed from my sister matched my dark, anxious mood. The mirrored disco ball hanging from the ceiling reflected light on the walls. The decorations dangling from above glistened like stars in the night sky. The gym, wrapped like a shiny present, was unrecognizable, though the air still smelled of sweat. Pop music blared from the DJ's speakers. Friends and classmates reveled in merriment.

I had been eagerly anticipating the sixth-grade spring dance all year. As the big day approached, it consumed every thought, action, and conversation of my friends. Amanda's mother was taking her into the city to buy a dress. Isabella's aunt was going to style her hair. Naomi's father said that she could splurge on a manicure. Alex announced that she was saving every dance for Devon Thomas. The more everyone babbled, the more anxious I became. The excessive talk added to my worries. What was I going to wear? Who would ask me to dance? I began to feel a tight knot in my stomach.

I soon spotted Amanda and Isabella standing by the tables of appetizers and desserts on the opposite side of the gym. I scurried around the perimeter of the dance floor to greet them. Amanda wore a short black-and-purple-striped dress with a shiny belt cinched at the waist. Isabella's hair was pulled up on top of her head, with loose curls cascading down like a waterfall. Naomi and Alex had already hit the dance floor. "Maria, you look fabulous!" Isabella gushed. I thanked my friend, grateful for her reassurance. Her comforting words made me feel less doubtful about the dance.

**INTRODUCTION** The writer captures the reader's attention with an interjection and then sets the scene by describing the setting and the way she feels about being there. Draw a star next to the word that the writer uses to grab the reader's attention. Box the words that show the writer's feelings.

**DETAILS** In paragraph 1, the writer uses details that appeal to the senses of sight, hearing, and smell to help the reader imagine the setting. Underline the details that describe the setting.

**POINT OF VIEW** Personal narratives are usually written in the first-person point of view. Underline the words that show the point of view.

**CONCLUSION** A good conclusion provides a reflection and describes a lesson the writer has learned or a change from the beginning of the story. At the end of the story, the writer reflects on the experience. Describe how the writer's feelings changed.

At first we huddled together, like an island in a storm, watching the revelry around us. Flushed and laughing, Alex and Devon joined us in between songs. Then Naomi arrived, completing our circle of friends. She was like a sportscaster providing a play-by-play of the hoopla around us. "John Hunt is dancing with Anne George. Look at the great dress Maria Lenova is wearing. Check out the group dancing together in the center of the floor. Rob DeMarco is strumming his invisible guitar again!" Surrounded by friends and fun, I began to relax.

After a while, a group of Devon's friends joined us. I didn't recognize them at first in their fancy dress pants, button-down shirts, stiff blazers, and shiny leather shoes. Then I realized that they looked as uncomfortable as I felt—like fish out of water. They squirmed in their unfamiliar apparel. One by one, Amanda, Isabella, Naomi, and Alex were asked to dance. The knot in my stomach turned into fluttering butterflies. Would I be next?

Out of the corner of my eye, I noticed Devon's best friend standing awkwardly nearby. I stepped toward him and blurted out, "Let's dance!" His face lit up as we walked onto the dance floor. Maybe the dance that I had worried about for so long was going to be all right, I thought.

At the beggining she was scared but at the end she wasn't scared and she was all right.

**Think About It ▶** Did the writer change or learn something from going to the dance? Did the writer use details to help the reader paint a picture in his or her mind?

## Vocabulary Study: Context Clues

**Context clues** are words, phrases, and sentences around unfamiliar words. You can often use these clues to figure out the meaning of an unfamiliar word. Work with your class or a partner to determine the meaning of each underlined word in the chart.

| Word in Context | Context Clues | Prediction |
|---|---|---|
| I <u>scanned</u> the large crowd several times, looking for my friends. | large crowd several times, looking | looked repeatedly or sweepingly at the crowd |
| Isabella's hair was pulled up on top of her head, with loose curls <u>cascading</u> down like a waterfall. | hair | |
| I thanked my friend, grateful for her <u>reassurance</u>. Her comforting words made me feel less doubtful about the dance. | | |

Look back at the personal narrative on pages 19–20. Find two unfamiliar words, and use context clues to predict their meanings. Write each word and your prediction in a box below. Then use a dictionary to check each word's meaning.

**Word**

**Predicted Meaning**

**Dictionary Meaning**

**Word**

**Predicted Meaning**

**Dictionary Meaning**

# Writing Process

Now that you have read and analyzed a personal narrative, you are going to create your own by following these steps of the writing process.

**1. Get Ready: Brainstorm** List several experiences you might want to write about. Choose the experience that seems most significant. Think about what you learned or how you changed. Think of details that will help the reader imagine the experience, and choose the most important ones.

**2. Organize** Use a graphic organizer to organize the sequence of events and to plan your personal narrative.

**3. Draft** Create the first draft of your personal narrative.

**4. Peer Review** Work with a partner to evaluate and improve your draft.

**5. Revise** Use suggestions from your peer review to revise your personal narrative.

**6. Edit** Check your work carefully for spelling, punctuation, and grammar errors.

**7. Publish** Create a final version of your personal narrative.

## Writing Assignment

In this lesson, you will write your own personal narrative. As you create the piece, remember the elements of the mentor text that were most effective. Read the following assignment.

> Write a personal narrative about a time you had to cope with bad weather, such as a blizzard, thunderstorm, hurricane, or tornado.
>
> Write at least five paragraphs describing your experience and showing how you faced and overcame fear.

# 1. Get Ready: Brainstorm

The first step in writing a personal narrative is to choose your topic. Begin by listing several topics related to the experience. List the significance of each.

Here's how the author of the mentor personal narrative brainstormed topics.

| Experience: Sixth-grade school dance | Significance |
|---|---|
| Topic: Getting ready for the dance | I felt grown up. |
| Topic: Worrying about not being asked to dance | I asked someone to dance and enjoyed myself after all. |
| Topic: Older brothers telling me that school dances are boring | I went to the dance anyway and had a good time. |

## Try It!  Use a Brainstorming Graphic Organizer

Now use the graphic organizer below to help you narrow your topic about coping with extreme weather for your personal narrative. Choose the topic you feel most strongly about.

| Experience: | Significance |
|---|---|
| Topic: | |
| Topic: | |
| Topic: | |

# Brainstorm Ideas for Your Narrative

You can use a graphic organizer to help brainstorm ideas and details for your personal narrative. Here is how the author of the mentor text used the graphic organizer.

**TOPIC** Select your topic and determine the focus for your personal narrative.

**Detail:** My friends were excited about the dance for a long time.

**Detail:** The gym was decorated. There was loud music.

**Detail:** When I arrived, I looked for my friends.

**Detail:** Everyone was talking about buying dresses, but I was getting scared.

**Topic:** My first school dance
**Focus:** I was excited at first but then got very anxious.

**Detail:** I could either be miserable or do something about it. I asked someone to dance.

**Detail:** My friends had all been asked to dance. I felt left out.

**Detail:** My friends and I watched everyone dance. We laughed and talked.

**Detail:** Devon's friends joined us. They were dressed up, too.

**DETAILS** Write down your memories of the event. Include your thoughts and feelings. You can add or revise details as you draft your personal narrative.

**CONCLUSION** Reflect on what you learned or how you changed. Include this detail in your brainstorming web.

# Try It!

**Use a Graphic Organizer for Brainstorming**

Now use the graphic organizer below to brainstorm ideas and details for your personal narrative.

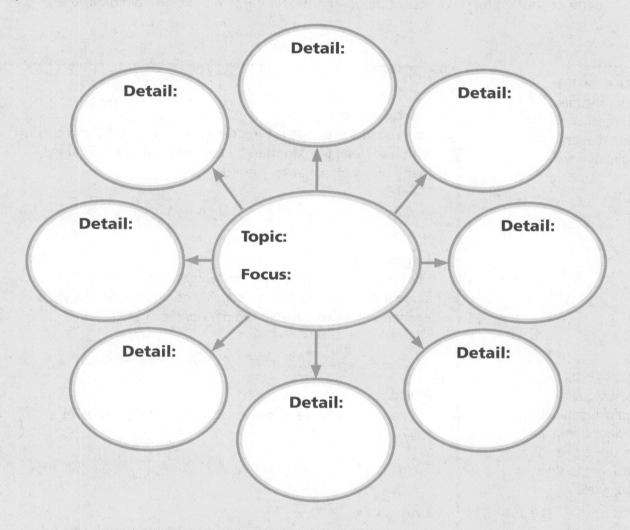

# 2. Organize

You are almost ready to begin a draft of your personal narrative. You can use a graphic organizer to help organize the event sequence and the details that you gathered during brainstorming. You can then refer to the graphic organizer as you work through different parts of your draft. The writer of the mentor text completed this graphic organizer.

**INTRODUCTION**
Grab the attention of the reader and establish the setting and point of view.

**BODY PARAGRAPHS** Use an event sequence that unfolds naturally, and include transition words. Use details and dialogue to show instead of tell.

**CONCLUSION**
Reflect on what you learned or how you changed.

**Introduction**
I arrived at the dance feeling nervous and noticed how the gym had been transformed by the decorating committee. Many of my classmates were dancing.

**Beginning**
My friends and I had been excited about the school dance since the beginning of the year. As the time drew closer, the excitement increased. So did my nerves.

**Middle**
I joined my friends and observed what was going on at the dance.

**End**
A group of boys joined us. Everyone began to pair off and dance. I asked a boy to dance, and he seemed happy to be asked.

**Conclusion**
After overcoming my fear and lack of confidence, I decided that I was going to enjoy the dance after all.

# Try It!

**Organize Your Personal Narrative**

Now use the graphic organizer below to organize the sequence of events and sensory details that you want to use in the different paragraphs of your draft.

**Introduction**

**Beginning**

**Middle**

**End**

**Conclusion**

# 3. Draft

Now it is time to begin the first draft of your personal narrative. Remember, your draft does not need to be perfect! This is the time to use your notes, get down your ideas in some sort of organized way, and have fun. You will have time to revise your writing later. Start by drafting your personal narrative on a computer or on a separate sheet of paper.

## Writer's Craft: Using Transition Words and Phrases

Transition words and phrases help writing flow smoothly. They can also help readers understand how the sequence of events are connected. Here are some common transition words and phrases.

| Transition words | first, next, finally, soon, afterward |
| --- | --- |
| Transition phrases | later that day, during the afternoon |

The author of the mentor text uses transition words and phrases in paragraph 5.

**TRANSITIONS**
Read this section of the mentor text. Underline the transition words and phrases that are used to move smoothly from one event to the next.

After a while, a group of Devon's friends joined us. I didn't recognize them at first in their fancy dress pants, button-down shirts, stiff blazers, and shiny leather shoes. Then I realized that they looked as uncomfortable as I felt—like fish out of water. They squirmed in their unfamiliar apparel. One by one, Amanda, Isabella, Naomi, and Alex were asked to dance. The knot in my stomach turned into fluttering butterflies. Would I be next?

# Try It! Write Your First Draft

On a computer or on a separate sheet of paper, complete the draft of your personal narrative. Remember to use transition words and phrases to connect one event to the next. Use this drafting checklist to help you as you write.

✓ Begin with an interesting sentence to grab the reader's attention, and describe the setting.

✓ Use the first-person point of view.

✓ Organize the event sequence so that it unfolds logically and naturally.

✓ Use descriptive details and dialogue.

✓ Use transition words and phrases to move smoothly from one event to the next.

✓ Provide a conclusion that follows from the narrated events. State what you have learned or how you have changed.

## Tips for Writing Your First Draft

- Determine the importance of the event before you begin your draft, and keep it in mind as you write.
- Remember that the events should be in order, but you can include a flashback to describe an event from the past.
- Use sensory details as well as dialogue to show, not tell, what the setting is like and what happens there.

# 4. Peer Review

After you finish your draft, you can work with a partner to review each other's drafts. Here is a draft of the mentor text. Read it with your partner. Together, answer the questions in the boxes. Then we'll see how the writer's classmate evaluated the draft.

**INTRODUCTION**
In the draft, the writer does not grab the reader's attention in the introduction. How might the writer make the beginning more interesting?

**BODY PARAGRAPHS**
Paragraph 3 could use dialogue. How would you add dialogue? Paragraph 4 could use some transitions. What words or phrases could you add?

**CONCLUSION** What thoughts and feelings would you add to this paragraph to show the significance of the change in how the writer felt when she asked Tim to dance?

## My First Dance!

I stood in the gym doorway. My black dress matched my mood. The mirrored disco ball hanging from the ceiling reflected light on the walls. The wall decorations sparkled like stars in the night sky. The gym was unrecognizable. Music blared from the DJ's speakers. Friends and classmates were dancing to the music.

I had been looking forward to the sixth-grade spring dance since the beginning of the school year. The dance was all my friends talked about. We talked about what we would wear. The more we talked about it, the more nervous I became.

I saw Amanda and Isabella standing on the other side of the room. I walked over to them. Naomi and Alex were dancing. Isabella told me that I looked beautiful. I felt a little better.

We stood there watching everything around us. Alex and Devon joined us in between dances. Naomi came over. She commented on the action around us. Surrounded by friends, I began to relax.

A group of Devon's friends joined us. I didn't recognize them at first. A few looked as uncomfortable as I felt like fish out of water. One by one, Amanda, Isabella, Naomi, and Alex were asked to dance. I felt the knot in my stomach begin to tighten.

I noticed Devon's friend Tim Smith standing nearby. I turned toward him and said, "Let's dance." We walked onto the dance floor together. The dance was going to be fun after all, I decided.

# An Example Peer Review Form

This peer review form gives an example of how a classmate evaluated the draft of the mentor text shown on the previous page.

| | |
|---|---|
| **The writer begins with an interesting lead sentence.** | You did a good job of *describing the setting.* |
| **The writer describes the setting in the first paragraph.** | You could improve your personal narrative by *making the first sentence more interesting to grab the reader's attention.* |
| **The writer organized the sequence of events to unfold logically and naturally.** | You did a good job of *organizing the sequence of events.* |
| **The writer uses transition words and phrases to make the writing flow smoothly.** | You could improve your personal narrative by *adding transitions.* |
| **The writer uses descriptive details that appeal to the senses.** | You did a good job of *including details to show the characters' behavior before the event.* |
| **The writer uses dialogue to develop the events and characters.** | You could improve your personal narrative by *adding dialogue to develop the events and characters.* |
| **The writer uses a conclusion that reflects on the experiences or events.** | You did a good job of *writing a conclusion that reflects on the narrated events.* |
| **The writer states what he or she learned or how he or she changed.** | You could improve your personal narrative by *adding more details to show how you felt.* |

# Try It!    Peer Review with a Partner

Now you are going to work with a partner to review each other's personal narrative drafts. You will use the peer review form below. If you need help, look back at the mentor text writer's peer review form for suggestions.

| | |
|---|---|
| **The writer begins with an interesting lead sentence.** | You did a good job of |
| **The writer describes the setting in the first paragraph.** | You could improve your personal narrative by |

| | |
|---|---|
| **The writer organized the sequence of events to unfold logically and naturally.** | You did a good job of |
| **The writer uses transition words and phrases to make the writing flow smoothly.** | You could improve your personal narrative by |

| | |
|---|---|
| **The writer uses descriptive details that appeal to the senses.** | You did a good job of |
| **The writer uses dialogue to develop the events and characters.** | You could improve your personal narrative by |

| | |
|---|---|
| **The writer uses a conclusion that reflects on the experiences or events.** | You did a good job of |
| **The writer states what he or she learned or how he or she changed.** | You could improve your personal narrative by |

# Try It!

**Record Key Peer Review Comments**

Now it is time for you and your partner to share your comments with each other. Listen to your partner's feedback, and write down the key comments in the left column. Then write some ideas for improving your draft in the right column.

| | |
|---|---|
| My review says that my introduction | I will |
| My review says that my use of sequence | I will |
| My review says that my use of details and dialogue | I will |
| My review says that my use of transitions | I will |
| My review says that my conclusion | I will |

Use the space below to write anything else you notice about your draft that you think you can improve.

# 5. Revise

In this step of the writing process, you work on parts of your draft that need improvement. Use the peer review form that your classmate completed to help you. You also use your own ideas about how to improve each part of your personal narrative. This checklist includes some things to think about as you revise.

**Revision Checklist**

✓ Do I begin with an interesting sentence to grab the reader's attention? Do I describe the setting in the introduction?

✓ Does the sequence of events flow in a logical manner? Do I use transitions to clarify the sequence and make the writing flow more smoothly?

✓ Do I use details and dialogue to show rather than tell?

✓ Do I reflect on what I learned or on how I changed as a result of the experience?

**PRECISE LANGUAGE**

Precise language means words or phrases that are clear and exact. Specific nouns, descriptive adjectives, and strong verbs create vivid images in a reader's mind. Look at the phrase *glistened like stars* in the sixth sentence. Would the word *shined* be more or less effective in this sentence? Why?

_____

_____

## Writer's Craft: Using Precise Language

Using precise words makes your writing clearer. Choose words that are specific and descriptive. For example, instead of using the word *walked*, you might use the word *trudged*. Now look at the mentor text for examples of precise language.

> Ugh! I paused nervously in the gym doorway at school. My heart was pounding as I scanned the large crowd several times, looking for my friends. The black dress and patent leather flats that I'd borrowed from my sister matched my dark, anxious mood. The mirrored disco ball hanging from the ceiling reflected light on the walls. The decorations dangling from above glistened like stars in the night sky. The gym, wrapped like a shiny present, was unrecognizable, though the air still smelled of sweat. Pop music blared from the DJ's speakers. Friends and classmates reveled in merriment.

# Try It!    **Revise Your Personal Narrative**

Replacing simple words or phrases with more descriptive or precise words is an important part of revising. Practice using precise language with the following paragraph. Write your answers on the lines below the paragraph.

> On my third day at Meadow School, I met three <u>nice</u> girls. They invited me to play a <u>game</u> with them after school. My mother was coming to get me in her <u>vehicle</u>, and I couldn't reach her. They agreed to <u>put off</u> the game until the weekend!

Replace *nice* with _____

Replace *game* with _____

Replace *vehicle* with _____

Replace *put off* with _____

## Writing Assignment

Continue working on a computer or on a separate sheet of paper. Review the assignment, repeated below, and the checklist. Doing so will help you know that you have included everything you need.

> Write a personal narrative about a time you had to cope with bad weather, such as a blizzard, thunderstorm, hurricane, or tornado.
>
> Write at least five paragraphs describing your experience and showing how you faced and overcame fear.

# 6. Edit

After revising your personal narrative, you will edit it. When you edit, you read very carefully to be sure you find and fix any mistakes in your writing. Here's a checklist of some things to look for as you edit.

---

**Editing Checklist**

✔ Did you indent each paragraph?

✔ Did you use complete sentences?

✔ Did you check for sentence fragments and run-on sentences?

✔ Did you use correct punctuation?

✔ Did you spell each word correctly?

---

You can use these editing marks to mark any errors you find.

| | | |
|---|---|---|
| # Add space | $\frac{|}{m}$ Insert em dash | ⹀ Add hyphen |
| ∿ Reverse order | ^ Insert | ⚲ Delete |
| ◯ Close up space | ˅ Insert apostrophe | |

This paragraph from the draft of the mentor text shows how to use editing marks.

A group of Devons friends joined us. I didnt reconize them at first. A few looked as uncomfortabell as I felt like fish out of water. One by one, Amanda Isabella Naomi, and Alex were asked to dance. I felt the not in my stomach begin to to tighten.

## Language Focus:
## Pronouns: Avoiding Shifts in Number or Person

**Pronouns** change form to show number (singular or plural), point of view (first, second, or third person), and gender (masculine or feminine).

Pronouns must agree in number with the nouns to which they refer. Singular pronouns refer to one person or thing (examples: I, me, it, you, he, she, his, hers, yours, someone, each). Plural pronouns refer to more than one (examples: we, us, they, them, theirs, ours, you, yours, everyone, everything).

Person refers to point of view or gender. First-person pronouns refer to the writer or speaker or to a group in which they belong (examples: I, me, we, us, mine, ours). Second-person pronouns refer to the audience of the writer or speaker (examples: you, yours). Third-person pronouns refer to anyone or anything else (examples: he, she, it, they).

Common grammatical errors include a shift in number or person. A writer or speaker might begin with a singular pronoun and mistakenly shift to a plural pronoun.

> Incorrect: <u>Someone</u> left the light on. <u>They</u> are irresponsible. (*Someone* is singular; *they* is plural.)
>
> Correct: <u>Someone</u> left the light on. <u>He or she</u> is irresponsible. (*Someone*, *he*, and *she* are singular.)

A writer or speaker might begin with a first-person pronoun and mistakenly shift to a second-person pronoun.

> Incorrect: <u>I</u> learned that <u>you</u> could take a train to Chicago. (*I* is first person; *you* is second person.)
>
> Correct: <u>I</u> learned that <u>we</u> could take a train to Chicago. (*I* and *we* are first person.)

Make sure that you do not mistakenly shift number or person when you use pronouns in your writing. Read the mentor text to find examples of pronouns.

> After a while, a group of Devon's friends joined us. I didn't recognize them at first in their fancy dress pants, button-down shirts, stiff blazers, and shiny leather shoes. They looked as uncomfortable as I felt—like fish out of water. They squirmed in their unfamiliar apparel. One by one, Amanda, Isabella, Naomi, and Alex were asked to dance. The knot in my stomach turned into fluttering butterflies. Would I be next?

**PRONOUNS** Personal pronouns can be singular or plural. They can also indicate point of view—first, second, and third person. Underline the pronouns in the mentor text. Circle the pronouns that indicate first-person point of view.

# Try It!  **Language and Editing Practice**

Underline the pronouns in each sentence. Then identify the person (*first, second,* or *third person*) and the number (*singular* or *plural*).

1. She delivered a speech on Tuesday. _____

2. We are expected to finish the homework on time. _____

3. You must work hard to earn a spot on the team. _____

4. They displayed tasteful work for the exhibit. _____

5. I am responsible for the mess. _____

Now use editing marks to correct pronoun shifts in number or person.

Everyone seemed to enjoy the school dance, including me. The students were

glad that the DJ played their favorite songs. We danced to it all evening. He or

she sang their favorite ones the top of their lungs. Somebody planned a dance

contest. Prizes were awarded. It was awarded to two students three times in a

row! The DJ presented the prizes to her. You could tell by looking at the rosy

cheeks and big smiles that he had a wonderful time!

# Try It!

**Edit Your Personal Narrative**

Now edit your personal narrative. Use this checklist and the editing marks you have learned to correct any errors you find.

- [ ] Did you indent each paragraph?

- [ ] Did you use complete sentences?

- [ ] Did you check for sentence fragments and run-on sentences?

- [ ] Did you use correct punctuation?

- [ ] Did you spell each word correctly?

- [ ] Did you use pronouns correctly?

- [ ] Did you use transitions effectively?

## Editing Tips

- Read your writing aloud. Add any missing words and correct any awkward sentences.

- Read over your writing several times. Each time, focus on something different. For example, focus on punctuation in one reading and spelling in another.

- Use precise language. Delete unnecessary words and phrases.

- Check your use of pronouns and point of view, making sure that they don't shift.

# 7. Publish

On a computer or a separate sheet of paper, create a neat final draft of your personal narrative. Correct all errors that you identified while editing your draft. Be sure to give your personal narrative an interesting title.

The final step is to publish your personal narrative. Here are some different ways you might choose to share your work.

- Read aloud your personal narrative to your class or to a small group of your classmates.

- Bind your personal narrative and the work of your classmates into a book for the classroom library.

- Submit your personal narrative for publication in your school newspaper.

- Create a classroom magazine with your personal narrative and those of your classmates. Make enough copies for each student in the class.

- Create a bulletin board displaying your personal narrative and the work of your classmates.

## Technology Suggestions
- **Upload your personal narrative onto your class Web site or blog.**
- **Combine your personal narrative with digital photos and print it out.**

# Reading Fiction

**Look at this** cave.

Why do you think explorers from the 1800s might have wanted to travel to the center of the Earth?

## ESSENTIAL QUESTION

*How can fiction bring imaginary events to life?*

**Consider ▶** What is the relationship between the narrator and his uncle?

Why is this chapter titled "A Woman's Courage"?

## CHAPTER VII:

# "A WOMAN'S COURAGE"

*The narrator is uncusy and distressed*

from *Journey to the Center of the Earth*
by Jules Verne

N

I came out of my uncle's study as if I had been stunned, and as if there was not air enough in all the streets of Hamburg to put me right again. . . .

Was I convinced of the truth of what I had heard? Had I not bent under the iron rule of Professor Liedenbrock? Was I to believe him in earnest in his intention to penetrate to the centre of this massive globe? Had I been listening to the mad speculations of a lunatic, or to the scientific conclusions of a lofty genius? Where did truth stop? Where did error begin? . . .

Shortly I espied my little Gräuben bravely returning with her light step to Hamburg.

"Gräuben!" I cried from afar off. . . .

5     "Axel!" she cried surprised. "What! have you come to meet me? Is this why you are here, sir?"

But when she had looked upon me, Gräuben could not fail to see the uneasiness and distress of my mind.

"What is the matter?" she said, holding out her hand. . . .

In a couple of minutes my pretty Virlandaise[1] was fully informed of the position of affairs. For a time she was silent. Did her heart palpitate as mine did? I don't know about that, but I know that her hand did not tremble in mine. We went on a hundred yards without speaking.

[1]**Virlandaise** a girl or young woman from Virland, Germany

> **MAKE INFERENCES/CITE EVIDENCE** When you make an inference, you use information you know and details from text to understand something that is not stated. How does the narrator feel about his uncle's idea to travel to the center of the Earth? What suggests this?

> **FIGURATIVE LANGUAGE** A figurative expression has a different meaning from the individual words used in it. Note the expression "iron rule" in paragraph 2. What does "iron rule" mean?

*Iron: HARD, TOUGH*

At last she said, "Axel! . . . That will be a splendid journey! . . . Yes, Axel, a journey worthy of the nephew of a savant;[2] it is a good thing for a man to be distinguished by some great enterprise." . . .

10 It was night when we arrived at the house. . . . I expected to find all quiet there, my uncle in bed as was his custom, and Martha giving her last touches with the feather brush.

But I had not taken into account the Professor's impatience. I found him shouting—and working himself up amidst a crowd of porters and messengers who were all depositing various loads in the passage. Our old servant was at her wits' end.

"Come, Axel, come, you miserable wretch," my uncle cried from as far-off as he could see me. "Your boxes are not packed, and my papers are not arranged; where's the key of my carpet bag?[3] . . .

[2]**savant** an educated person

[3]**carpet bag** a type of suitcase or duffle bag

Charatzation
1. Looks
2. actions     5. Thoughts +
3. Words            feelings
4. Wotas

**COMPARE AND CONTRAST TEXTS** To compare things is to point out similarities, and to contrast things is to point out differences. Compare and contrast what you've read in this selection so far with information you might read in a science article about Earth's layers.

**AUTHOR'S GEOGRAPHIC LOCATION** Jules Verne was born in France. How do you think residing in Europe influenced his perspective in this story?

**CHARACTERS** Characters are the people, animals, or other creatures in a story. A writer reveals a character's traits by describing how the character looks and acts, what the character thinks and says, and the way other characters react to him or her. How would you describe the narrator's character and his relationship with his uncle?

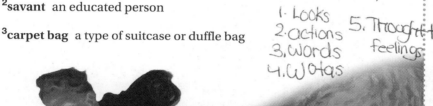

I stood thunderstruck. My voice failed. Scarcely could my lips utter the words:

"Are we really going?"

15 "Of course, you unhappy boy! Could I have dreamed that you would have gone out for a walk instead of hurrying your preparations forward?"

"Are we to go?" I asked again, with sinking hopes.

"Yes; the day after to-morrow, early."

I could hear no more. I fled for refuge into my own little room.

All hope was now at an end. My uncle had been all the morning making purchases of a part of the tools and apparatus required for this desperate undertaking. The passage was encumbered with rope ladders, knotted cords, torches . . . grappling irons . . . pickaxes, enough to load ten men.

20 I spent an awful night. Next morning I was called early. . . .

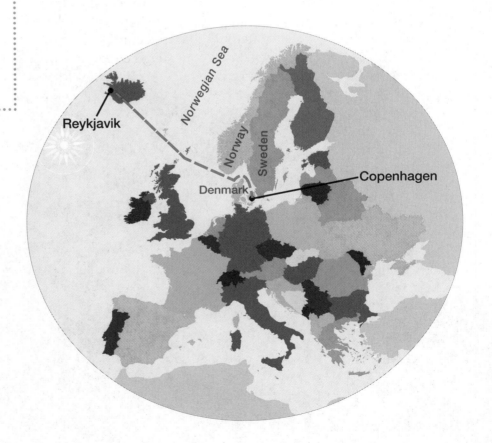

"Uncle, is it true that we are to go?"

"Why do you doubt?"

"Well, I don't doubt," I said, not to vex him; "but, I ask, what need is there to hurry?"

"Time, time, flying with irreparable rapidity."

25 "But it is only the 16th May, and until the end of June—"

"What, you monument of ignorance! Do you think you can get to Iceland in a couple of days? . . . There is only one trip every month from Copenhagen to Reykjavik, on the 22nd."

"Well?"

"Well, if we waited for the 22nd June we should be too late. . . . Therefore we must get to Copenhagen as fast as we can to secure our passage. Go and pack up."

There was no reply to this. I went up to my room. Gräuben followed me. She undertook to pack up all things necessary for my voyage. She was no more moved than if I had been starting for a little trip. . . . Her little hands moved without haste. She talked quietly. She supplied me with sensible reasons for our expedition. She delighted me, and yet I was angry with her. Now and then I felt I ought to break out into a passion, but she took no notice and went on her way as methodically as ever.

30 Finally the last strap was buckled; I came downstairs. All that day the philosophical instrument makers and the electricians kept coming and going. Martha was distracted.

"Is master mad?" she asked.

I nodded my head.

"And is he going to take you with him?"

I nodded again.

35 "Where to?"

I pointed with my finger downward.

"Down into the cellar?" cried the old servant.

"No," I said. "Lower down than that."

**POINT OF VIEW/NARRATOR**
A story's point of view is the perspective of the narrator of the story. If the story is told in first-person point of view, it is told by one of the characters using the pronouns *I* and *me.* If the story is told in third-person point of view, it is told by someone outside the story and uses such pronouns as *he, she, it,* and *they.* What is the point of view of this chapter? Who is the narrator?

WORD CHOICE AND TONE
An author carefully chooses words to set the tone of a passage. The tone is the author's attitude toward a topic. Note the use of the word *decreed* in paragraph 40. Why does the author choose to use this word? How does this affect the tone of the passage?

CONTEXT CLUES  Context clues are nearby words and phrases that help you figure out the meaning of an unknown word. What context clues help you determine the meaning of the word *inert*?

USE REFERENCE SOURCES
A reference source, such as a dictionary, thesaurus, or glossary, can help you understand the meanings of words as you read. What reference source would be the best choice for finding the definition of *multifarious*? Why?

Night came. But I knew nothing about the lapse of time.

40     "To-morrow morning at six precisely," my uncle decreed, "we start."

At ten o'clock I fell upon my bed, a dead lump of inert matter. All through the night terror had hold of me. I spent it dreaming of abysses. I was a prey to delirium. I felt myself grasped by the Professor's sinewy hand, dragged along, hurled down, shattered into little bits. I dropped down unfathomable precipices with the accelerating velocity of bodies falling through space. My life had become an endless fall. I awoke at five with shattered nerves, trembling and weary. I came downstairs. My uncle was at table, devouring his breakfast. I stared at him with horror and disgust. But dear Gräuben was there; so I said nothing, and could eat nothing.

At half-past five there was a rattle of wheels outside. A large carriage was there to take us to the Altona railway station. It was soon piled up with my uncle's multifarious preparations.

"Where's your box?" he cried.

"It is ready," I replied, with faltering voice.

45     "Then make haste down, or we shall lose the train."

It was now manifestly impossible to maintain the struggle against destiny. I went up again to my room, and rolling my portmanteaus[4] downstairs, I darted after him.

---

[4] **portmanteaus**  large suitcases

At that moment my uncle was solemnly investing Gräuben with the reins of government. . . . She kissed her guardian; but could not restrain a tear in touching my cheek with her gentle lips.

"Gräuben!" I murmured.

"Go, my dear Axel, go! I am now your betrothed; and when you come back I will be your wife."

50     I pressed her in my arms and took my place in the carriage. Martha and the young girl, standing at the door, waved their last farewell. Then the horses, roused by the driver's whistling, darted off at a gallop on the road to Altona.

**PREDICT AND CONFIRM MEANING** When you don't recognize a word, you can make an assumption about what it means based on story details. If you don't recognize the word *betrothed*, what can you guess it means? How can you confirm the meaning of the word *betrothed*? Explain.

**THEME** A story's central message is its theme. A theme usually expresses a larger truth about human nature or society. Think about the characters and action in this chapter. What theme do they suggest? What details support this theme?

**SUMMARIZE** A summary is a restatement of the main events in a text. Summarize the events in this chapter.

## Comprehension Check

Look back in "A Woman's Courage" to note Axel's dialogue, thoughts, actions, and reactions to others. Use the graphic organizer to formulate three adjectives that accurately describe Axel.

| Example of Axel's Dialogue, Thoughts, Actions, Reactions | Adjective that Describes Axel |
|---|---|
| A. Had I been listening to the mad speculations of a lunatic, or to the scientific conclusions of a lofty genius? | curious, concerned |
| B. | |
| C. | |

D. Why is the chapter titled "A Woman's Courage"?

_____

_____

_____

## Vocabulary

Use the word map below to help you define and use one of the highlighted vocabulary words from the Share and Learn selection you are about to read or another word you chose.

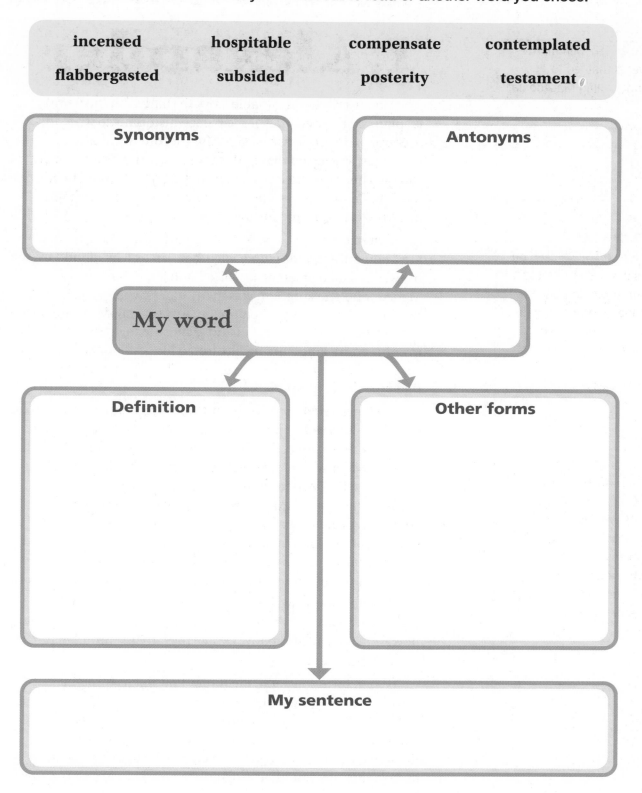

incensed    hospitable    compensate    contemplated

flabbergasted    subsided    posterity    testament

**Synonyms**

**Antonyms**

**My word**

**Definition**

**Other forms**

**My sentence**

**Consider ▶** Why is the setting important to Alexander's behavior?

What lesson does Alexander teach to the other characters?

**SUMMARIZE** Summarize the events that led to Alexander ruling Macedonia.

_____

_____

_____

**MAKE INFERENCES/ CITE EVIDENCE** Based on details in the story, would it be appropriate to state that Alexander is conceited? Cite evidence to support your inference.

_____

_____

_____

**WORD CHOICE** Alexander uses the word _rigorous_ in paragraph 4 to describe his daily exercise. Why do you think the author used this word instead of a word like _healthy_ or _vigorous_?

_____

_____

_____

# I, Alexander

1    I knew I had a formidable story to share with the world. I'd planned to direct one of the palace historians to write the account of the impressive events for me, but my mother, Olympias, suggested that I, Alexander, write it myself. It is my story, so perhaps she is correct in stating that I should be the one to tell it. Before I begin, though, I must provide background information regarding my life.

I often do not see eye to eye with my father, King Philip. We are frequently at odds with each other. That's why I found myself truly astonished when he departed and left me in charge of Macedonia. The kingdom was in my hands when he left for Byzantium to quash a rebellion. I'm just sixteen. My mother said that by making me his regent and giving me the power to rule over his entire kingdom, he illustrated his confidence in me. I suspected that he was setting me up to fail, so I pledged to myself that I would do a superlative job.

I felt prepared to assume control. My father had always made certain I had the best possible education. Even though I often argued with Aristotle, the Greek philosopher my father hired to be my teacher when I was thirteen, I did appreciate all the knowledge I'd gleaned from him insofar as rhetoric, literature, science, medicine, and philosophy. I particularly enjoyed conversing with him about my favorite book, Homer's _Iliad_. Reading about the Trojan War and the deeds of my ancestor, the famous warrior Achilles, provided the driving force behind my desire to pursue battle and demonstrate my courage to the world.

I'm not simply well educated. I also engage in rigorous exercise every day, as I recognize the importance of a king being powerful in mind and body. I know my father is proud of me for my skill as an equestrian.

5    When I was fourteen, the trader Philonicus brought a warhorse named Bucephalus to the palace to sell. The price he demanded was thirteen talents, which my father determined was outrageous. He challenged Philonicus by explaining that the horse would have to prove itself worthy before such an outrageous sum could be exacted.

As Bucephalus gleamed in a stream of sunlight with his mane blowing in the wind, I thought he was the most majestic horse I had ever seen. Philonicus mounted him to demonstrate the horse's skills, but Bucephalus reared and dashed him to the ground. Several of my father's attendants also attempted to ride Bucephalus, and all of them were tossed off as though they had the weight of a feather. My father was incensed, but I was closely noting the events to deduce the problem and determine how to make the horse more hospitable to a rider. "I can manage that horse," I proclaimed.

"You think you can mount a horse that threw a master equestrian such as Philonicus?" my father scoffed. "What would you be willing to wager that you can succeed where others have failed?"

"If I can ride Bucephalus," I said firmly, "you will purchase him for me. If I cannot ride him, I will compensate you with thirteen talents."

**ANALOGY** The author describes the men trying to ride Bucephalus as having the weight of a feather. What does this analogy tell you about the horse?

_____

_____

_____

**CHARACTERS** How does Alexander's father react when Alexander claims he can mount the horse?

_____

_____

_____

**POINT OF VIEW**
Is "I, Alexander" told from
the same point of view as "A
Woman's Courage"? Explain.

_____

_____

**ADAGE/PROVERB**
Underline the context clues
that point to the meaning
of the adage "An ounce of
observation is worth a
pound of force."

**PLOT** After Alexander
becomes ruler of Mace-
donia, he has to crush a
rebellion. What similar
event happens earlier in
the passage?

_____

_____

**THEME** What lesson do you
learn from reading this story?

_____

_____

**COMPARE AND
CONTRAST TEXTS** What
is the genre of this passage?
How does it compare with
"A Woman's Courage"?

_____

_____

When I contemplated the expressions of those around me,
I knew the crowd was filled with skeptics. But I was confident. I
slowly approached the horse, speaking to him in gentle tones.
Then I turned him around. Seconds later, I mounted him, and
without incident, we galloped around the field.

10  As my father paid for Bucephalus, I explained to my
flabbergasted audience that I had observed the horse's behavior
and realized he was shying away from his own shadow. "An
ounce of observation is worth a pound of force," I proclaimed.
Once I moved the horse so he was facing the sun, he could no
longer see his shadow, so his fear subsided. My father shook his
head and remarked, "My son, you will have to find another
kingdom; Macedonia is too small for you!"

Maybe it was this episode that convinced him to trust
me with his kingdom. I'm keenly aware that it provided the
confidence I needed to take action when the Thracians in the
northern part of our kingdom revolted soon after my father left
me in charge. My mother agonized about my safety, but I knew
my training had prepared me for the battle at hand. Without
hesitation, I gathered troops and marched to Thrace. We easily
crushed the rebellion, and then I established a colony that I
named Alexandroupoli—after myself.

I, Alexander, know I will be a great king. Now that I have
distinguished myself in battle and proven myself a daring leader,
perhaps my father will agree. This is my story. I have written it
down in my own words for posterity—so the story will serve as
a testament to my early greatness.

## Anchor Standard Discussion Questions

Discuss the following questions with your peer group. Then record your answers in the space provided.

1. What motivates Alexander? Support your answer with details from the text.

_____

_____

_____

_____

_____

_____

2. How does the point of view from which "I, Alexander" is told affect your opinion of him? Would your opinion of Alexander be different had the palace historian (mentioned in paragraph 1) told the story instead? Support your answer with details from the text.

_____

_____

_____

_____

_____

_____

## Comprehension Check

1. How do "A Woman's Courage" and "I, Alexander" approach similar themes and topics?

_____

_____

_____

2. Based on what happened in the story, what do you think is Alexander's view of how to resolve conflicts?

_____

_____

_____

3. If you were to write a new adage or proverb based on "I, Alexander," what would it be? Why?

_____

_____

_____

### Read On Your Own

Read another story, "The Lucky Teakettle," independently. Apply what you learned in this lesson and check your understanding.

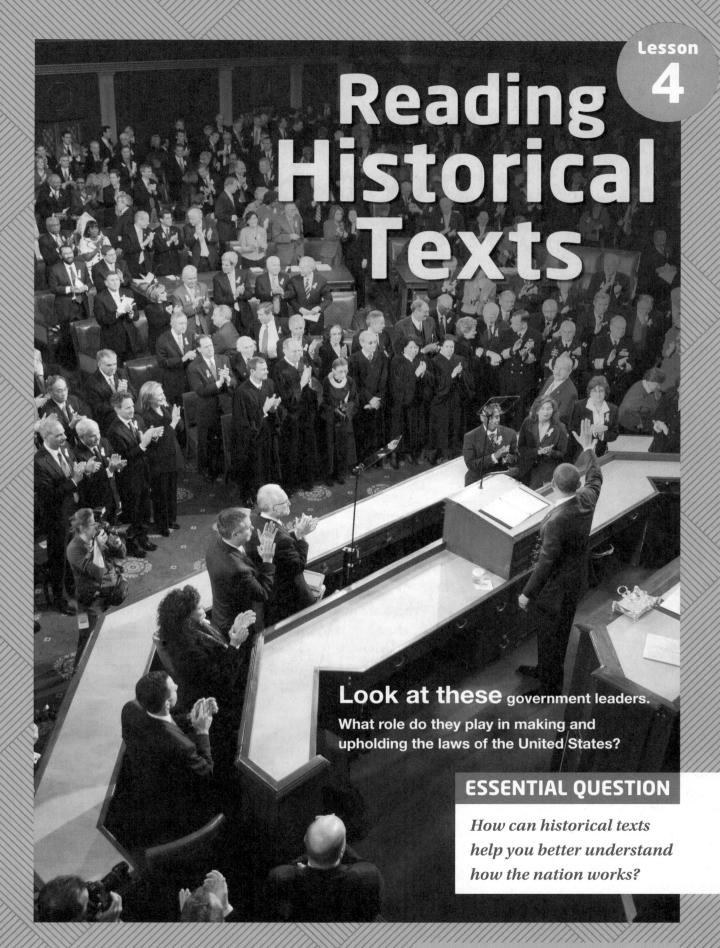

# Reading Historical Texts

**Look at these** government leaders.
What role do they play in making and
upholding the laws of the United States?

## ESSENTIAL QUESTION

*How can historical texts
help you better understand
how the nation works?*

**Consider ▶** Why is a detailed process required for a bill to become law?

Why is it important to know how to contact your legislators?

# How a Bill Becomes a Law

**This is the hopper in the U.S. House of Representatives.**

1 *There ought to be a law!* Have you ever had this thought? Maybe you'd like to see a law passed to declare a new national holiday. Perhaps you'd like to get the ball rolling on a law that would make all school supplies free. Is the ball in your court? Can you—or anyone at all in the country—come up with an idea for a new law?

Yes! But only a member of the United States Congress—the House of Representatives or the Senate—can introduce a bill to get the ball rolling for a new U.S. law. All people, though, can contact their congressional representatives or senators to share their ideas and ask that a bill be introduced.

Though bills can be introduced in the Senate, most bills are introduced in the House of Representatives, so let's first take a look at the process of how a bill becomes a law in the House of Representatives. Then you can read a flowchart to note some major differences in the process as it unfolds in the Senate.

There are many steps in the process for a bill to become a law. Most bills never make it far enough through the steps to become law. As you'll see while you're reading about the process, there are many opportunities for a bill to die before it ever reaches the point of becoming a law. Read on to see what determines whether a bill lives or dies.

**Introducing the Bill: Toss It into the Hopper**

5 The very first step in the passage of a new law is the introduction of a bill in Congress. The bill is simply the idea proposed for a new law, in writing. A member of Congress introduces the bill by tossing it into the hopper. "Hopper" is a lively name for a box that is provided for just this purpose. Each bill that finds its way into the hopper is rewarded with its own identifying number. This makes it easy to track the bill as it travels through Congress.

> **HISTORICAL TEXTS** Historical texts include true and accurate facts about laws, social customs, and events from the past. Why can the information about how a bill becomes law be identified as historical text?

### Committee Action: Pull It from the Hopper

Congress is filled with committees. They each focus on an important area, such as education, the workforce, budget, energy, or commerce. Members of the appropriate committee discuss the bill after it has been pulled from the hopper. Some bills are sent to a specialized subcommittee. Most bills fail to journey beyond the committee step. When this happens, it is said that a bill "does not make it out of committee." It dies. Often, bills are killed because it's decided that they don't address an issue important enough to warrant a law. They are also frequently killed because research into the bill shows that there are serious problems with it, and so it should not move forward to become a law.

### Reporting the Bill: Send It Forward

After considering a bill, a committee can release the bill with a report that describes its purpose and why it was recommended for approval. Then the bill makes its way to a calendar that schedules floor action.

### Taking Floor Action: Examine It

After the bill is reported, it is ready to be examined through floor action. This is a formal examination of the bill by members of Congress. This examination can include debate and discussion.

**TEXT STRUCTURE** Analyzing text structure can help you understand the information in a passage. Some examples of text structure are *sequence*, which describes events or steps in time order; *comparing and contrasting*, which tells how items are similar and different; and *cause and effect*, which shows how one or more events occur as a result of other events. Which two types of text structure can you find in "How a Bill Becomes a Law"? Explain.

**STEPS IN A PROCESS** When you tell the steps in a process, you recognize and state the key steps that must be taken to complete an action or arrive at a goal. Does reporting a bill happen before or after taking floor action? Does reporting a bill happen before or after placing the bill in the hopper?

10    For some bills, debate and discussion are short. For others, debate and discussion can grow quite lively and last a while. Congressional debates are often televised, so it's possible to watch the debates and listen to the opinions of representatives and senators. It's also possible to contact these legislators through e-mail, so you can let your own representatives and senators know your thoughts about whether or not you think a specific bill should pass.

**Voting: Put It to the Test**

After floor discussion, the bill is put up for a vote. Members of Congress are permitted to place one of three votes: "yea" for yes, "nay" for no, or "present." If a member of Congress votes "present," this means the member is present during the vote but abstains, or chooses not to vote. If the bill does not pass in Congress, it dies.

**Enrollment: Send It on to the President**

If the bill passes in Congress, it is sent to the president, where a variety of actions are possible:

- If the president signs the bill, it becomes law.
- If the president ignores the bill, it becomes law within ten days if Congress is in session. If Congress is not in session, the bill dies. This is called a pocket veto.
- If the president vetoes the bill, two-thirds of Congress can override the veto. If this happens, the bill becomes law.

## How a Bill Becomes Law: An Overview of the Steps

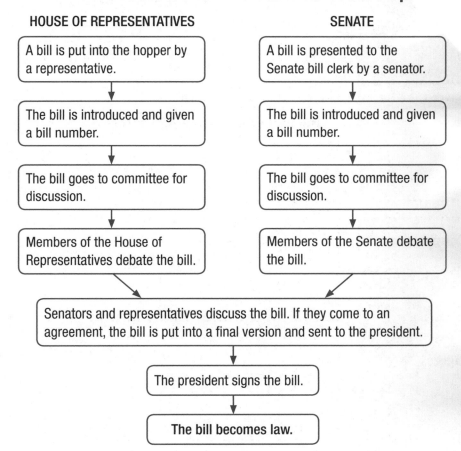

HOUSE OF REPRESENTATIVES

SENATE

A bill is put into the hopper by a representative.

A bill is presented to the Senate bill clerk by a senator.

The bill is introduced and given a bill number.

The bill is introduced and given a bill number.

The bill goes to committee for discussion.

The bill goes to committee for discussion.

Members of the House of Representatives debate the bill.

Members of the Senate debate the bill.

Senators and representatives discuss the bill. If they come to an agreement, the bill is put into a final version and sent to the president.

The president signs the bill.

The bill becomes law.

**SOCIAL STUDIES VOCABULARY** What is the meaning of *veto*? Why is this an important social studies term? What is the meaning of *override*? Why is this an important social studies term?

**KEY DETAILS** The process for making laws is detailed and precise. It requires Congress and the president to follow certain steps for specific scenarios. What is a pocket veto? What happens if the president vetoes a bill? How can Congress override the president's veto?

**SUMMARY** In a summary, you restate information in a shortened form—often no more than a few sentences—in your own words. A summary focuses on the main ideas, or the most important information, in a passage. Provide a summary of the enrollment process.

**GRAPHICS** Graphics are visual representations of information that can improve your understanding of what you read. This graphic is a flowchart, showing the steps in a process. What does this graphic represent? Why are the column labels and arrows important?

## Comprehension Check

Use information from "How a Bill Becomes a Law" to complete the empty boxes in the cause-and-effect chart.

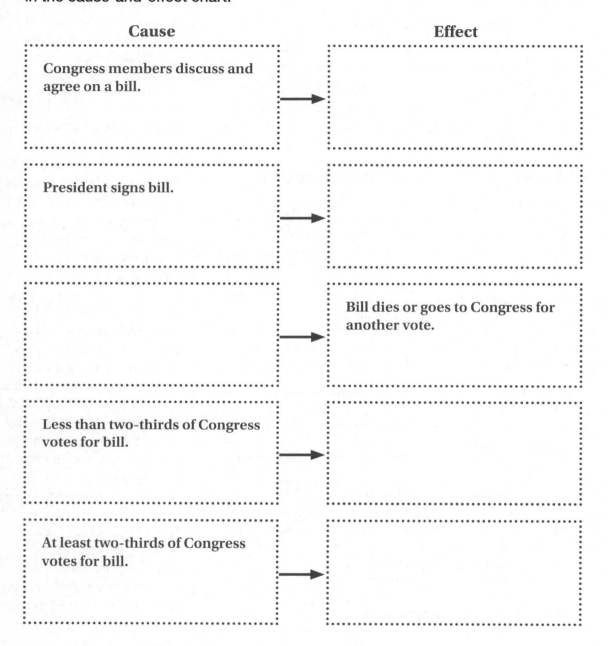

**Cause**

**Effect**

Congress members discuss and agree on a bill.

President signs bill.

Bill dies or goes to Congress for another vote.

Less than two-thirds of Congress votes for bill.

At least two-thirds of Congress votes for bill.

## Vocabulary

Use the word map below to help you define and use one of the highlighted vocabulary words from the Share and Learn selection you are about to read or another word you choose.

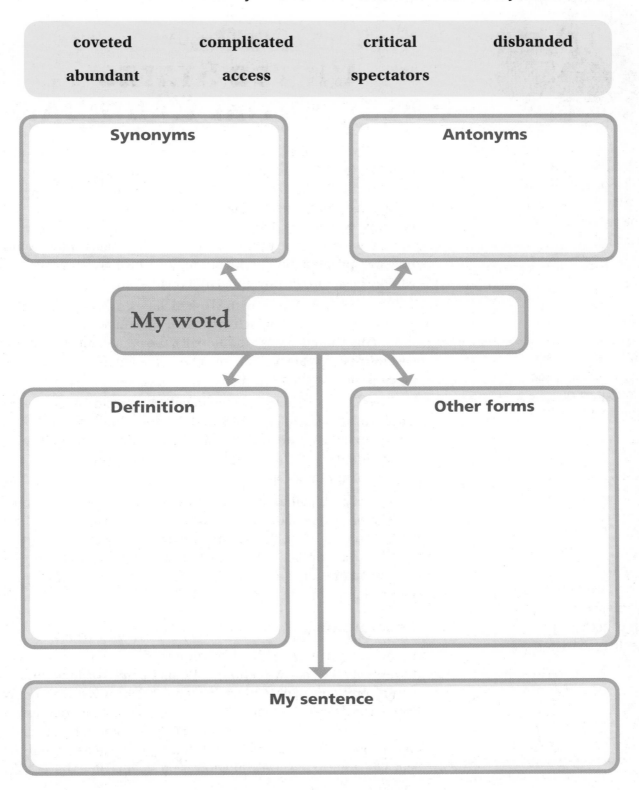

coveted          complicated          critical          disbanded

abundant          access          spectators

**Synonyms**

**Antonyms**

My word

**Definition**

**Other forms**

**My sentence**

**Consider ▶**

How difficult is it to become a presidential candidate?

What role do states play in the process of nominating a presidential candidate?

## HOW TO BECOME A
# UNITED STATES PRESIDENTIAL CANDIDATE

**ROOTS AND AFFIXES**
What does *extraordinary* mean? How do the word parts help you figure out the meaning?

_____

_____

**CONTEXT CLUES** What does *unanimously* mean? How do context clues help you figure out the meaning?

_____

_____

**SOCIAL STUDIES VOCABULARY** What does the word *delegates* mean? Why is this word important to understanding the process of becoming a presidential candidate?

_____

_____

1    Do you have big dreams? Is there an extraordinary goal you would like to achieve in life? Many people dream of becoming president of the United States. The road to this coveted office is a long but exciting one. It's filled with many twists and turns, but many people imagine that it's certainly worth the trip. The process of electing the president of the United States has become more complicated throughout our nation's history. Let's start with the basics to see how to set foot on this path.

To serve as president of the United States, a person must be a natural-born citizen, which means the person must have been born in the United States. Additionally, the person must be at least thirty-five years old and must have lived in the United States for at least fourteen years.

To understand how a person becomes a presidential candidate, it's critical to understand the role of political parties. Throughout the decades, there have been a number of political parties. Many have disbanded, but two major parties—and a number of minor ones—still exist.

It's very difficult to become a presidential candidate without the support of one of the major parties, the Democratic Party or the Republican Party. These parties provide abundant support to a presidential candidate, including funding, opportunities to easily send messages and ideas to many people, and access to research and workers.

### Historical Changes

5    Selecting a president has become an increasingly complex process over the past two centuries. When George Washington became president of the United States in 1789, he was unanimously selected by delegates to attend the Second Continental Congress. All the delegates agreed that he should become president. At that time, people designated by the states simply came together and held a meeting to select Washington as president. Times have certainly changed.

## State Primaries and Caucuses

Before a candidate can run for president, he or she must be chosen by a political party. Each state holds a primary or a caucus for this purpose during an election year, which occurs every four years. Most states hold primaries. In a caucus, party members have meetings and give speeches to support specific candidates; then they vote to select a candidate. In a primary, voters come to the polls to vote for a specific candidate.

In state primaries and caucuses, party members vote for the presidential candidate who they believe best represents their particular party. Based on the results in the primaries and caucuses, delegates are sent to vote for and select the party's candidate at the national convention.

The delegates to the Democratic National Convention chose Barack Obama (above) as their nominee for president in 2008. The delegates to the Republican National Convention chose John McCain (right) as their nominee.

**CITE EVIDENCE** Is it more or less difficult to become a presidential candidate now than it was during the time of George Washington? Use examples from the passage to support and explain your response.

_____

_____

_____

**CENTRAL IDEA** Circle the paragraph that best states the central idea of the passage.

**STEPS IN A PROCESS** What is the first step in becoming a presidential candidate?

_____

_____

_____

**TEXT STRUCTURE** What are the causes of sending delegates to vote for and to select a party's candidate at the national convention?

_____

_____

_____

Suppose you wanted
to find a synonym for
*national*. Which resource—
a dictionary, a glossary, or
a thesaurus—would be
the best choice to use?

_____

_____

_____

**SUMMARY** Write a
summary of the steps in
the process of becoming
the presidential nominee
of a political party.

_____

_____

_____

**GRAPHICS** Draw an arrow
to the map that shows
the results of the 2008
Republican primary. Circle
the map that shows the
results of the 2008
Democratic primary. Who
won the 2008 Republican
presidential nomination?
Name two states that this
candidate won. Who won
the 2008 Democratic
presidential nomination?
Name two states that this
candidate won.

_____

_____

_____

### National Convention

Each major political party holds a national convention
during an election year. Delegates from each state in the country
attend the convention. These delegates are chosen in each state
based on rules set by the political party and the state. The
delegates place the formal votes for the party's candidate.

The candidate who receives the majority of the delegates'
votes becomes the party's candidate for the office of the president
of the United States. In 2008, the major Republican candidates
were John McCain, Mitt Romney, and Mike Huckabee. For the
Democratic Party, the main candidates were Barack Obama and
Hillary Clinton. McCain won the Republican nomination, and
Obama won the Democratic nomination.

10    National conventions are often bustling events attended
by thousands. Delegates are passionate about supporting
their candidates. These conventions are televised, which gives
spectators around the world the opportunity to watch democracy
in action, as Americans decide who will run for the presidency.

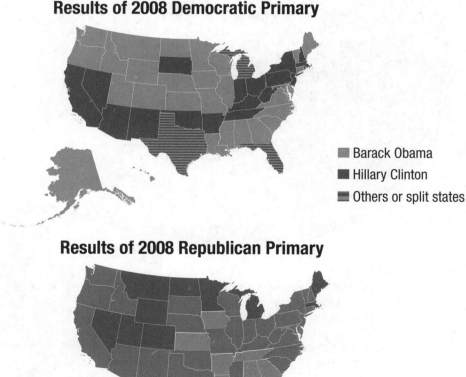

**Results of 2008 Democratic Primary**

- Barack Obama
- Hillary Clinton
- Others or split states

**Results of 2008 Republican Primary**

- John McCain
- Mitt Romney
- Mike Huckabee

## Anchor Standard Discussion Question

**Discuss the following question with your peer group. Then record your answer in the space provided.**

1. Every piece of writing has a tone, including an article about the road a candidate must take to become president. What is the author's attitude toward the subject of the article? Support your answer using details from the text.

_____

_____

_____

_____

_____

_____

_____

_____

_____

_____

_____

## Comprehension Check

1. How would you summarize "How to Become a United States Presidential Candidate"?

_____

_____

_____

2. Why is it generally believed that a candidate needs the support of one of the major political parties to gain a presidential nomination? Cite evidence from "How to Become a United States Presidential Candidate" to support your response.

_____

_____

_____

3. How do the maps help you to better understand "How to Become a United States Presidential Candidate"? Support your response with specific examples.

_____

_____

_____

## Read On Your Own

Read another historical text, "The Impeachment Process," independently. Apply what you learned in this lesson and check your understanding.

# Writing Fictional Narratives

## ESSENTIAL QUESTION

*How do setting, plot, and characters make an effective fictional narrative?*

**Storytelling** is a form of entertainment and a method of conveying information that people of all ages have enjoyed for centuries. Think about a story that captured your interest. Where and when did the story take place? What problem or conflict did the characters have to resolve? Now think of a story you could write in which the characters face a challenge at sea.

# What's a Fictional Narrative?

Have you thought about what it might be like to have an encounter at sea? Maybe the encounter would involve risk or danger, or it could just be a new experience. You can use your imagination to write a fictional narrative about someone who faces a challenge or difficulty at sea.

A **fictional narrative** is a made-up story in which the setting, characters, and/or events may be realistic or based on fantasy. The story may be told from the first-person point of view, using the pronoun *I*, or from the third-person point of view, using pronouns such as *he*, *she*, and *they*.

**Introduction**
Introduce the main characters and the setting. Describe the problem, or conflict, in the story, and establish the narrative point of view.

**Plot**
Create events that build tension toward the climax, or the most suspenseful part of the story. Use action and dialogue to show how the character or characters try to overcome the problem.

**Climax**
Make this part of the story suspenseful and exciting. Tell how your character finally solves the problem.

**Conclusion/Resolution**
Show what happens after the climax. Tell how the conflict or problem is solved.

Let's look at a fictional narrative.

## Analyze a Mentor Text

This is an example of an effective fictional narrative by a sixth grader. Read it and then complete the activities in the boxes as a class.

### Dugong Rescue

"Do we have to go so slowly?" Tim complained as his uncle, Sid, carefully steered their motorboat around outcroppings of coral. "We could see more of the Great Barrier Reef if you went faster."

"You could see more if you just looked," insisted Tim's sister Julia, gazing down at the multicolored fish swimming through the water.

Julia and Tim were in Australia visiting their uncle, Sid, who was a marine biologist, a scientist who studies sea animals. He was taking them snorkeling out at the reef. They couldn't wait to swim underwater themselves with the colorful fish.

"We have to go slowly so the propeller doesn't accidentally injure a dugong (DOO•gong)," explained Uncle Sid.

"What's a dugong?" asked Julia. "Is it another species of fish?"

"No, a dugong's a sea mammal," explained Uncle Sid.

"So are they like dolphins and whales?" asked Tim.

"Close," said Uncle Sid, "but dugongs can't hold their breath underwater for as long as those other sea mammals."

"Maybe we'll see one," said Julia hopefully.

"That's unlikely," said Uncle Sid. "People rarely get to see dugongs, except in captivity."

"So what exactly do they look like?" Julia asked.

"They look something like giant seals," said Uncle Sid. "Some dugongs are about nine feet long and weigh more than eight hundred pounds."

"They're silvery gray and have a large snout," added Tim. "There's one right over there!"

**INTRODUCTION** The writer sets the scene in the first three paragraphs. Underline the setting. Circle the names of the characters.

**DIALOGUE** Dialogue is used to *show* rather than *tell* the reader about the dugong. The characters compare and contrast the dugong with other marine life they are familiar with, which helps the reader understand what a dugong is. Draw boxes around those facts that you learned about the dugong through the characters' dialogue.

Julia turned and exclaimed, "It's bigger than our boat!"

Uncle Sid quickly shut off the motor, and they drifted close enough to the dugong to see its round head and small eyes.

Suddenly, the dugong started thrashing and screaming in the water.

"What's wrong with it?" Julia sounded worried.

"It's tangled in a net!" Tim exclaimed.

Uncle Sid grabbed his mask and dove over the side of the boat.

Julia and Tim put on their masks, snorkels, and flippers. When they dove into the water, they could see that one of the dugong's fins was caught in a fishing net. They watched as Uncle Sid took a knife from his ankle sheath. He was about to cut the net when the dugong jerked and knocked the knife from his hand. The knife sank. Uncle Sid and Tim kept trying to loosen the net with their bare hands. But the net wrestled Uncle Sid for control of the dugong.

Meanwhile, Julia rose to the surface and took a deep breath. She placed her tongue over the mouthpiece to keep water from leaking through the snorkel. Then she dove down after the knife. Something glittered on the ocean floor a few feet away. It was the knife!

Julia had just enough breath left to grab the handle and rise to the surface. She swam as fast as she could toward Uncle Sid and Tim. Then she tapped Uncle Sid on the shoulder and handed him the knife. He cut the net, setting the dugong free. Julia watched the dugong rise to the surface to breathe, smile, and then swim away.

"What was that fishing net doing there?" Tim asked after they had all climbed back into their boat.

"Sometimes fishing nets break loose and drift into places they shouldn't be," said Uncle Sid. "That dugong was lucky. If we hadn't seen it, it would have drowned in that net."

"I think we were the lucky ones," said Julia. "We got to see a dugong!"

**Think About It ▶** Did the writer use setting and plot effectively to make the reader want to keep reading the story?

## Vocabulary Study: Figurative Language

Figurative language includes similes, metaphors, and personification, among others. Writers use **personification** when they apply human qualities to something that is not human, such as an animal or object. Writers use personification for effect. They may use it to make a story more interesting or a poem more dramatic. Look at the following examples.

**1.** *The sea is angry.*

What emotion does this sentence convey? The sea is not literally angry, but the reader gets a sense that waves are violently crashing in the sea.

**2.** *The wind danced in the trees.*

What emotion does this sentence convey? Wind does not literally dance in the trees, but the reader gets a sense that the leaves of the trees were rhythmically moving or swaying as the wind blew by them.

Look back at the fictional narrative on pages 69–70. Find two examples of personification. Write them in the chart below, as well as their meanings.

| Example: | Example: |
| --- | --- |
| **Meaning:** | **Meaning:** |

# Writing Process

Now that you have read and analyzed a fictional narrative, you are going to create your own by following these steps of the writing process.

**1. Get Ready: Brainstorm** List several ideas you have for settings, characters, and plot. Choose the setting, characters, and plot that are the most interesting to you. Brainstorm details about them. Think of a problem the character or characters experience. Choose plot events that might lead to the problem, and then think of a solution.

**2. Organize** Use a graphic organizer to organize the sequence of events and details in the plot.

**3. Draft** Create the first draft of your fictional narrative.

**4. Peer Review** Work with a partner to evaluate and improve your draft.

**5. Revise** Use suggestions from your peer review to revise your fictional narrative.

**6. Edit** Check your work carefully for errors in spelling, punctuation, and grammar.

**7. Publish** Create a final version of your fictional narrative.

## Writing Assignment

In this lesson, you will write your own fictional narrative. As you create the piece, remember the elements of the mentor text that were most effective. Read the following assignment.

> Write your own fictional narrative about an encounter at sea. Make sure your narrative has a setting, a plot, and well-developed characters.

# 1. Get Ready: Brainstorm

When you brainstorm, you think of as many ideas as you can. Start by making a chart like the one below and filling in the first column with ideas about an encounter at sea. This will help you choose your topic. Then think about the characters, setting, and problem.

Here's how the writer of the mentor fictional narrative brainstormed ideas.

| Ideas: An encounter at sea | Characters | Setting | Problem |
| --- | --- | --- | --- |
| sailboat race | captain and crew | Lake Michigan | There is severe weather. |
| whale-watching cruise | mother, father, three children | Alaska | Whales thrash about, making waves near the boat. |
| snorkeling | uncle, niece, and nephew | Great Barrier Reef, Australia | They find a dugong trapped in a fishing net. |

## Try It!

**Use a Brainstorming Graphic Organizer**

Now use the graphic organizer below to help brainstorm ideas for your own fictional narrative.

| Ideas: An encounter at sea | Characters | Setting | Problem |
| --- | --- | --- | --- |
| | | | |
| | | | |
| | | | |

# Brainstorm Ideas for Your Narrative

You can use a graphic organizer to help brainstorm ideas and details for the topic of your fictional narrative. Here is how the writer of the mentor text used a web.

**CHARACTERS**
List characters and include details about the relationships between them.

**SETTING** Select details about the setting in which your narrative takes place. For example, some readers might not know what the Great Barrier Reef is like, so the mentor text writer listed some details about it.

**PROBLEM/PLOT**
Include details about what the main problem will be and what events will occur around that problem.

**RESOLUTION**
Include details about what happens after the climax and how the problem is solved.

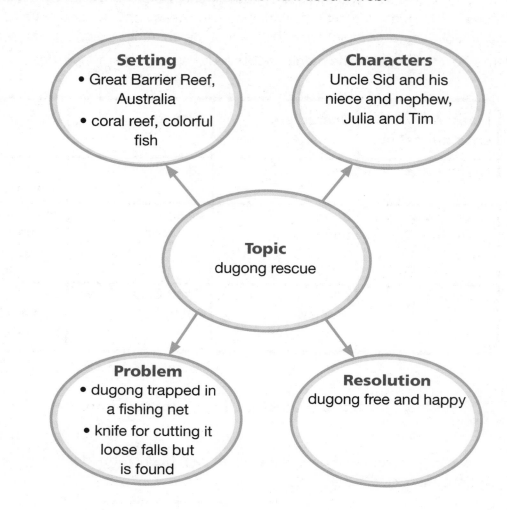

**Setting**
- Great Barrier Reef, Australia
- coral reef, colorful fish

**Characters**
Uncle Sid and his niece and nephew, Julia and Tim

**Topic**
dugong rescue

**Problem**
- dugong trapped in a fishing net
- knife for cutting it loose falls but is found

**Resolution**
dugong free and happy

# Try It!

**Use a Graphic Organizer for Brainstorming**

Now use the web below to brainstorm details for your fictional narrative.

**Setting**

**Characters**

**Topic**

**Problem**

**Resolution**

# 2. Organize

You are almost ready to begin a draft of your fictional narrative. You can use a graphic organizer to help develop the ideas and details that you gathered during brainstorming. You can then refer to the graphic organizer as you work through the different parts of your draft. The writer of the mentor text completed this graphic organizer.

## INTRODUCTION
Be sure to

- set the scene/grab interest
- build background
- introduce characters/setting

## PLOT/PROBLEM
Be sure to

- describe the problem
- describe how the characters solve it

## CLIMAX
Be sure to

- describe the most exciting events
- use descriptive language/dialogue
- create a point of greatest tension before the problem is solved

## RESOLUTION
Be sure to

- describe events after the climax
- tell how the problem is solved

---

### Introduction

- Uncle Sid, a marine biologist, is taking his niece and nephew, Julia and Tim, snorkeling in Australia's Great Barrier Reef.

- Tim is eager to get there. Uncle Sid explains that they have to go slowly so that the propeller doesn't injure a dugong. He explains what a dugong is.

### Plot/Problem

1. Uncle Sid, Julia, and Tim see a dugong trapped in a fishing net.

2. They put on their masks, flippers, and snorkels and jump into the water to try to rescue the dugong.

3. Uncle Sid takes out a knife to cut the net.

### Climax

- The dugong struggles, which causes Uncle Sid to drop his knife.

- Tim and Uncle Sid try to free the dugong from the net.

- Julia finds the knife.

### Resolution

- Uncle Sid cuts the net.

- The dugong swims away.

## Try It!

**Organize Your Fictional Narrative**

Now use the graphic organizer below to organize the ideas, sequence of events, and descriptive details you want to use in your draft.

**Introduction:**

**Plot/Problem:**

**Climax:**

**Resolution:**

# 3. Draft

Now it is time to write the first draft of your fictional narrative. Remember, your draft does not have to be perfect. This is the time to use your notes and get your ideas down in an organized way. You will have time to revise your writing later.

## Writer's Craft: Using Dialogue

You can use **dialogue**, or the words of the characters, to show what they are like and to move the action forward. Dialogue can also be a way to provide more information to the reader.

The author of the mentor text uses dialogue to give information about the setting and to show that Tim is impatient and eager to see the Great Barrier Reef.

> "Do we have to go so slowly?" Tim complained as his uncle, Sid, carefully steered their motorboat around outcroppings of coral. "We could see more of the Great Barrier Reef if you went faster."

Now read this section of dialogue from the mentor text.

**DIALOGUE**
Underline the dialogue in this section of the text. Does the dialogue effectively move the story forward? How?

> Suddenly, the dugong started thrashing and screaming in the water.
>
> "What's wrong with it?" Julia sounded worried.
>
> "It's tangled in a net!" Tim exclaimed.
>
> Uncle Sid grabbed his mask and dove over the side of the boat.

# Try It!    **Write Your First Draft**

On a computer or on a separate sheet of paper, complete the draft of your fictional narrative. Use this drafting checklist to help you as you write.

 A good introduction grabs the reader's attention. You can begin with a question, an announcement, or an exclamation to make the reader want to continue reading.

 Follow your story map, and use descriptive language and sensory details.

 Balance your fictional narrative with dialogue, action, and narration.

 Organize the event sequence so that it unfolds logically and naturally.

 Build toward the climax, and make it exciting.

## Tips for Writing Your First Draft

- Start writing to get your ideas down. You will revise your draft later.
- Develop the characters, setting, and problem that you identified while brainstorming.
- Write about the events in chronological order. You can add more details and descriptive text later.
- Use sensory details to help the reader experience what you are describing.

# 4. Peer Review

After you finish your draft, you can work with a partner to review each other's drafts. Here is a draft of the mentor text. Read it with your partner. Together, answer the questions in the boxes. Then we'll see how the writer's classmate evaluated the draft.

**DEVELOP SETTING AND CHARACTERS**
The writer does a good job of setting the scene but does not make it clear how Uncle Sid knows about marine life. What information should be added?

**CLIMAX** How would you revise the draft so that the tension builds toward the climax and the narrative *shows*, rather than *tells*, what happens?

**RESOLUTION**
The conclusion does not show how the problem was resolved. How could the author wrap up the story better? How could dialogue and details make the ending more interesting?

## Dugong Rescue!

"Do we have to go so slowly?" Tim said. His uncle Sid steered their motorboat around the Great Barrier Reef. His sister, Julia, was looking at the fish swimming nearby.

Julia and Tim were visiting their uncle Sid in Australia. He was taking them snorkeling out at the reef.

"We have to go slowly so the propeller doesn't injure a dugong (DOO•gong)," said Uncle Sid.

"What's a dugong?" asked Julia. "Is it a species of fish?"

"No, a dugong is a sea mammal," said Uncle Sid. "They can't hold their breath under water as long as dolphins. People rarely get to see dugongs, except in captivity."

"So what exactly do they look like?" Julia asked.

"They look something like giant seals," said Uncle Sid. "Some dugongs are about nine feet long and weigh more than eight hundred pounds. They're silvery gray and have a large snout."

Tim pointed over the side of the boat. "There's one!"

The dugong started thrashing in the water. It was tangled in a net. Uncle Sid dove over the side of the boat. Julia and Tim followed him. One of the dugong's fins was caught in the fishing net. Uncle Sid took a knife from his ankle sheath. The dugong jerked and knocked the knife from his hand.

Julia dove down after the knife. If she couldn't find it, the dugong would drown! She saw something on the ocean floor a few feet away. Julia grabbed the knife and rose to the surface. She handed Uncle Sid the knife.

"That dugong was lucky," said Uncle Sid. "If we hadn't seen it, it would have drowned in that net."

# An Example Peer Review Form

This peer review form gives an example of how a classmate evaluated the draft of the mentor text shown on the last page.

| | |
|---|---|
| **The introduction sets the scene and grabs the reader's interest.** | You did a good job of *setting the scene and grabbing my interest through dialogue.* |
| **The writer introduces the setting, characters, and/or problem.** | You could improve your fictional narrative by *adding details to make the problem clearer and more dramatic.* |

| | |
|---|---|
| **The writer uses dialogue to make the characters come alive or to move the action forward.** | You did a good job of *using dialogue to show what the characters are like.* |
| **The writer uses descriptive details to develop the characters and setting.** | You could improve your fictional narrative by *adding more descriptive details to the setting.* |

| | |
|---|---|
| **The writer creates a sense of tension through descriptive details and a clear sequence of events.** | You did a good job of *organizing the sequence of events.* |
| | You could improve your fictional narrative by *adding details that help build tension.* |

| | |
|---|---|
| **The writer shows how the problem is solved.** | You did a good job of *using dialogue after the problem was solved.* |
| **The conclusion wraps up the story with clear details and/or dialogue.** | You could improve your fictional narrative by *using more descriptive details to describe what happened after the problem was solved.* |

# Try It!

**Peer Review with a Partner**

Now you are going to work with a partner to review each other's fictional narrative drafts. You will use the peer review form below. If you need help, look back at the mentor text writer's peer review form for suggestions.

| | |
|---|---|
| **The introduction sets the scene and grabs the reader's interest.** | You did a good job of |
| **The writer introduces the setting, characters, and/or problem.** | You could improve your fictional narrative by |
| **The writer uses dialogue to make the characters come alive or to move the action forward.** | You did a good job of |
| **The writer uses descriptive details to develop the characters and setting.** | You could improve your fictional narrative by |
| **The writer creates a sense of tension through descriptive details and a clear sequence of events.** | You did a good job of |
| | You could improve your fictional narrative by |
| **The writer shows how the problem is solved.** | You did a good job of |
| **The conclusion wraps up the story with clear details and/or dialogue.** | You could improve your fictional narrative by |

# Try It!    **Record Key Peer Review Comments**

Now it is time for you and your partner to share your comments with each other. Listen to your partner's feedback, and write down the key comments in the left column. Then write some ideas for improving your draft in the right column.

| | |
|---|---|
| My review says that my introduction | I will |
| My review says that the problem or conflict | I will |
| My review says that the events | I will |
| My review says that the climax of the story | I will |
| My review says that the resolution | I will |

Use the space below to write anything else you notice about your draft that you think you can improve.

# 5. Revise

In this step of the writing process, you work on parts of your draft that need improvement. Use the peer review form that your classmate completed to help you. Also use your own ideas about how to improve each part of your fictional narrative. This checklist includes some things to think about as you get ready to revise.

> **Revision Checklist**
>
> ✓ Does the introduction grab the reader's attention? Do I set the scene clearly?
>
> ✓ Do I use details and dialogue to make my story come alive?
>
> ✓ Do I tell the events in a logical order and build tension?
>
> ✓ Do the characters solve the problem in a way that is believable?
>
> ✓ Do I explain what happens after the problem is solved? Is the resolution clear?

**SENSORY LANGUAGE**

Underline the details in these paragraphs that appeal to the senses. Look at the sentences describing the dugong. How do the words paint a picture in your mind? Why is it more effective than saying "Julia saw the dugong come up for air"?

_____

_____

_____

## Writer's Craft: Using Sensory Language

Sensory language tells what something looks, sounds, feels, smells, and even tastes like. Using sensory language helps draw readers into a scene, making them feel as if they are actually there. Now look at the mentor text for examples of sensory language.

Julia turned and exclaimed, "It's bigger than our boat!"

Uncle Sid quickly shut off the motor, and they drifted close enough to the dugong to see its round head and small eyes.

Suddenly, the dugong started thrashing and screaming in the water.

# Try It!

**Revise Your Fictional Narrative**

Using sensory details is an important part of revising. Sensory language helps you to show, rather than tell, what is happening in your story. Revise the paragraph below by adding sensory details. Write your answers on the lines provided.

> Waiting for the bus to arrive, Kim and her older sister felt glad they had dressed for rain. Although it was raining, they were protected. Finally, the bus drove up, and the girls climbed on and found two seats in the middle. They enjoyed looking out the windows and studying the storefronts whenever the bus stopped. They were almost sorry when they reached the building that housed their music classes.

_____

_____

_____

_____

## Writing Assignment

Continue working on a computer or on a separate sheet of paper. Review the assignment, repeated below, and the checklist. Doing so will help you make sure that you have included everything you need.

> Write your own fictional narrative about an encounter at sea. Make sure your narrative has a setting, a plot, and well-developed characters.

# 6. Edit

After revising your fictional narrative, you will edit it. When you edit, you read very carefully to find any mistakes in your writing. Here's a checklist of some things to look for as you edit.

---

**Editing Checklist**

✔ Did you indent each paragraph?

✔ Did you write clear, complete sentences?

✔ Did you combine short, choppy sentences?

✔ Did you punctuate all dialogue correctly?

✔ Did you use correct capitalization and end punctuation?

✔ Did you spell each word correctly?

---

You can use these editing marks to correct any errors you find.

| | |
|---|---|
| ◯ Close up space | # Add space |
| ˆ Insert comma | ¶ Begin new paragraph |
| ⸗ Add hyphen | ⹂ ⹂ Insert quotation marks |

This paragraph from the draft of the mentor text shows how to use editing marks.

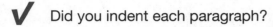

"So what exactly do they look like? Julia asked. They look something like giant seals, said Uncle Sid. "Some du gongs are about nine feet long and weigh more than eight hundred pounds. They're silvery gray and have a large snout."

# Language Focus: Pronoun Case and Intensifiers

Writers use pronouns to refer to people or things that have already been mentioned or to emphasize nouns or pronouns. A **pronoun** is used in place of a noun. The accurate use of subject pronouns, object pronouns, possessive pronouns, and intensive pronouns will make your writing more effective.

**Subject Pronouns**—I, you, we, he, she, it, they—are used as subject or predicate nouns:

> Correct: *She* is a good writer.
> Incorrect: *Her* is a good writer.

**Object Pronouns**—me, you, us, it, him, her, them—are used as direct objects, indirect objects, or objects of prepositions:

> Correct: The actor gave *them* an autograph.
> Incorrect: The actor gave *they* an autograph.

**Possessive Pronouns**—his, hers, yours, mine, theirs, ours, its—take the place of possessive nouns:

> Example: My shoes are newer than your shoes.
> *Mine* are newer than *yours*.

**Intensive Pronouns**—myself, yourself, yourselves, himself, herself, itself, oneself, ourselves, themselves—emphasize a noun or pronoun and end with -*self* or -*selves*. Not all pronouns ending with -*self* or -*selves* are intensive pronouns. Intensive pronouns call attention to the noun or nouns they accompany.

> Example: *I* built the birdhouse *myself*.
> (Notice that *myself* emphasizes *I*.)

Now read the mentor text below to find examples of subject, object, possessive, and intensive pronouns.

> Julia and Tim were in Australia visiting their uncle, Sid, who was a marine biologist, a scientist who studies sea animals. He was taking them snorkeling out at the reef. They couldn't wait to swim underwater themselves with the colorful fish.

**INTENSIVE PRONOUNS**
Use pronouns to replace nouns that have already been used and to emphasize nouns or pronouns. Underline the pronouns in this paragraph. Circle the intensive pronoun. Which noun or pronoun does it emphasize?

# Try It!   **Language and Editing Practice**

Underline the pronoun in each sentence. Then write *subject*, *object*, *possessive*, or *intensive* on the line provided.

1. Janice mailed it at the post office. _____

2. She hoped the contest entry would arrive on time. _____

3. Mr. Dean said that it was due by Friday. _____

4. Janice hoped hers would be the winner. _____

5. Janice wrote the fictional narrative herself. _____

**Now use editing marks to correct the errors in this paragraph.**

Mr. Lyons explained the rules for the upcoming student council elections

and everyone listened intently. "Candidates are required to give a speech

about them qualifications for the job", noted Mr. Lyons. "Our class will listen to

the speechs on Monday.

# Try It!

**Edit Your Fictional Narrative**

Now edit your fictional narrative. Use this checklist and the editing marks you have learned to correct any errors you find.

☐ Did you indent each paragraph?

☐ Did you start a new paragraph each time a different speaker said something?

☐ Did you use complete sentences?

☐ Did you spell each word correctly?

☐ Did you use pronouns correctly?

☐ Did you use correct capitalization and punctuation?

## Editing Tips

- Read your writing aloud. Add any missing words. Ask yourself, "Does this sound right?"

- Review how to use commas and quotation marks when writing dialogue. Reread your writing to make sure you have used commas and quotation marks correctly.

- Ask a classmate or family member to read your narrative aloud. Listen for any parts that do not sound right. You may need to add punctuation or rewrite a sentence or paragraph.

# ⑦ Publish

On a computer or on a separate sheet of paper, create a neat final draft of your fictional narrative. Correct all errors that you identified while editing your draft. Give your fictional narrative an interesting title.

The final step is to publish your fictional narrative. Here are some different ways you might choose to share your work.

- Read your fictional narrative to the class or to a small group of students.

- Create a poster to publicize your fictional narrative and to capture the attention of readers.

- Submit your fictional narrative for publication in your school newspaper.

- Create a cover, title page, and dedication page. Bind the final draft of your fictional narrative into book form. Make a copy to donate to your classroom or school library.

## Technology Suggestions

- Upload your fictional narrative to a class Web site or blog.
- Incorporate digital photographs into your final draft.
- Save your fictional narrative in PDF format so it can be e-mailed to family and friends.

# Reading Drama

## Look at this astronaut.

What feelings do you think this astronaut is experiencing as he prepares for spaceflight?

## ESSENTIAL QUESTION

*How can drama help you better understand the feelings and viewpoints of characters?*

**Consider ▶** How can readers understand a character in drama?

What features in dramatic literature help readers understand what they are reading?

# MISSION TO MARS

## Cast of Characters

*Marla Schmidt (astronaut on the Pluvius)*

*Daniel Lewis (astronaut on the Pluvius)*

*Oscar Diaz (head of Mission Control)*

### Act 1
### Scene 1

*(Schmidt and Lewis are onstage in chairs that represent the cockpit of a space shuttle.)*

1 **Diaz:** *(from offstage; voice piped in through speaker)* This is Control. Prepare for countdown.

**Schmidt:** Lewis, what do you think? A pretty momentous occasion, isn't it? Ready to be one of the first two humans to step foot on Mars?

**Lewis:** To tell you the truth, I've dreamed of a moment like this since I was a kid. I grew up thinking that people would never get to go to Mars, but now here I am, about to go on one of the most historic space missions of all time.

**Schmidt:** I read you loud and clear. I couldn't have expressed those thoughts better myself. And it's amazing to think that the whole world is watching us as we head toward the Red Planet.

5 **Diaz:** *(from offstage; voice piped in through speaker)* We are go for launch. Let the countdown start. 10, 9 . . . *(quietly, in background behind Schmidt's voice)* 8, 7, 6 . . .

**Schmidt:** *(with an air of confidence and authority in her voice)* Just think of all that preparation we went through. Soon it will seem as though infinity is out there, just beyond this capsule.

**Diaz:** *(from offstage; voice piped in through speaker)* 5, 4, 3, 2, 1 . . . Liftoff!

*(Schmidt and Lewis lean back as if from the force of liftoff.)*

**Lewis:** *(laughing)* Whoa! Liftoff is a lot bumpier than I'd expected! Are all systems functioning? Please check.

**Schmidt:** Check. All systems are operative. Let's reassess after we jettison the booster rockets.

10 **Diaz:** *(from offstage; voice piped in through speaker)* *Pluvius*, it appears there's a problem. One of the booster rocket controls is stuck. We're seeing a glitch in the automatic system. Stand by. We're working toward an alternate solution now. *(Pause)* Okay, *Pluvius*, you'll have to release manually. Do you copy?

**Schmidt:** Copy that, Control. Moving to manual now.

**ELEMENTS OF DRAMA**
A drama is usually broken into several acts, which are then broken into scenes. Often each scene will have a different setting, or location where the action takes place. What is the setting of Scene 1? How can you tell?

**PLOT** Plot is the series of events that make up a story. It includes a problem or central conflict and the events that lead to its resolution. What is the central conflict in Scene 1?

**CHARACTER** Stage directions and dialogue help to develop the characters in a play. What does the stage direction in paragraph 14 reveal about Lewis? How does Schmidt respond to reassure Lewis? How do you know that Lewis is reassured?

**Lewis:** *(to Schmidt)* Failure to release as scheduled could drag us down.

**Schmidt:** *(flipping switches)* Affirmative, Lewis, but if we release too soon, we won't have enough fuel to complete the mission. We can handle this—just the way we handled it in training.

**Lewis:** *(looking concerned as he manipulates levers and buttons and reads controls)* We've got 30 seconds . . . 20 . . . 10 . . .

15 **Schmidt:** *(calmly, with authority)* Hang in there, Lewis . . . and . . . RELEASE!

**Lewis:** *(looking relieved)* Confirming: booster rockets have been released. Repeat: booster rockets are away. Whew!

**Diaz:** *(from offstage; voice piped in through speaker)* Good job, *Pluvius!*

## Scene 2

*(Many months later, aboard the* Pluvius, *Schmidt and Lewis are looking sleepy.)*

**Diaz:** *(from offstage; voice piped in through speaker)* Good morning, *Pluvius*! Ready for the big day?

**Lewis:** *(yawns and rubs his eyes)* It's morning already? Tough to tell up here!

20 **Diaz:** *(from offstage; voice piped in through speaker; sounds elated)* It's definitely morning down here. And you're about to see what no human has ever seen before.

**Schmidt:** *(watching, amazed, through a window)* Look at that! It's phenomenal! Our first Martian sunrise! *(extended pause)* Okay now, let's get moving, Lewis. It's going to be a big day!

**ELEMENTS OF DRAMA**
Why is the drama divided into two scenes?

## Comprehension Check

In a drama, the stage directions and the dialogue work together to show the characters' movements, thoughts, and feelings. Choose a character, a line of dialogue, and the stage direction for the dialogue. Enter the information in the chart, and then tell what the dialogue and stage direction together reveal about the character.

| A. Character | Stage directions | Line of dialogue |
|---|---|---|
| Lewis | (looking concerned as he manipulates levers and buttons and reads controls) | We've got 30 seconds . . . 20 . . . 10 . . . |

What is revealed about the character: Lewis is afraid that the rockets will not release as planned.

| B. Character | Stage directions | Line of dialogue |
|---|---|---|
|  |  |  |

What is revealed about the character:

| C. Character | Stage directions | Line of dialogue |
|---|---|---|
|  |  |  |

What is revealed about the character:

| D. Character | Stage directions | Line of dialogue |
|---|---|---|
|  |  |  |

What is revealed about the character:

## Vocabulary

Use the word map below to help you define and use one of the highlighted vocabulary words from the Share and Learn selection you are about to read or another word you choose.

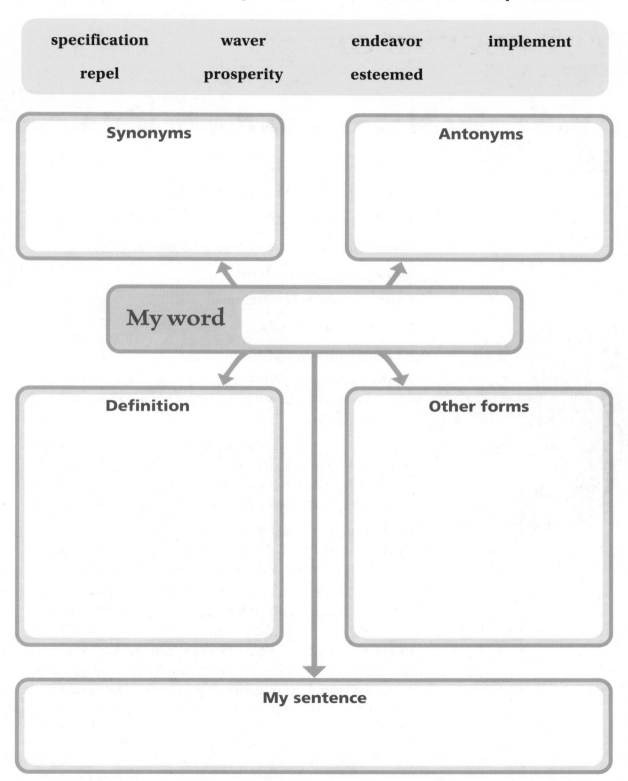

specification    waver    endeavor    implement

repel    prosperity    esteemed

**Synonyms**

**Antonyms**

My word

**Definition**

**Other forms**

**My sentence**

**Consider ▶** Why is Arthur able to pull the sword from the stone?

What is the importance of Merlin to King Arthur and Uther Pendragon?

# THE LEGEND OF KING ARTHUR

## Cast of Characters

*Arthur, rightful heir to the throne*

*Merlin, advisor to King Uther and King Arthur*

*King Uther Pendragon, king of England*

*Nanny, caregiver to Arthur*

*Randolph, friend to Arthur*

*Edward, young knight*

*Richard, young knight*

*Walton, young knight*

### ACT 1
### Scene 1

*(King Uther is lying in bed as he is dying. Merlin sits beside him. In the background, Nanny holds an infant wrapped in blankets. A very tall sword in a sheath stands in a corner of the room.)*

1 **King Uther:** *(weakly)* Merlin, I fear my time is near. My country is at war. My people are dying. I wish to serve them, to protect them, but I know my hours on this Earth are numbered.

**Merlin:** *(taking Uther's hand and speaking in a firm but soothing tone)* Uther, there is one more important arrangement to be made.

**King Uther:** I know, I know. Our kingdom may fall, but I feel confident that it will rise up again. And it will need a ruler, a ruler who is kind, who cares for all the subjects, who is able to bring together our country and protect it from those who would assail it.

**Merlin:** *(glancing back at Nanny and the baby)* What shall we do about Arthur, your son? He is heir to the throne. He is the only one who may rightfully take it one day.

5   **King Uther:** *(clutching Merlin's coat and speaking in stage whisper)* Whisk my Arthur away to safety, Merlin. Watch over him. Guide him.

**Merlin:** You know I shall honor your wishes.

**King Uther:** *(weakly pointing to the sword standing in the corner of the room)* When the time is right, make certain Arthur takes the sword Excalibur. Make haste to return him to his claim, his rightful place on the throne.

*(Uther closes eyes and lies still; it is clear he has died.)*

**Merlin:** *(walking solemnly to Nanny and the baby and handing a packet to Nanny, then speaking urgently)* Take Arthur. Hide him as we discussed.

**Nanny:** *(nodding as she takes the packet and holds the baby close)* I shall do as you told me in the specifications. I will not waver in my responsibility to our future king. But how will I know when the time is right? How will I tell Arthur he is the rightful heir to the throne?

10   **Merlin:** You shall never tell him! Such knowledge would place him in grave danger. He shall grow up as any peasant child. I shall come to him often—as his friend. When the time is right, I shall guide him to Excalibur.

**Nanny:** *(scurrying away with the baby)* As you wish, Merlin.

**ELEMENTS OF DRAMA**
Why is including the baby in Scene 1 important to the plot?

_____

_____

_____

**MAKE INFERENCES**
What inference can you reasonably make about the type of care Merlin has arranged for Arthur? Can you reasonably infer that Merlin believes Arthur will be safe? Explain.

_____

_____

_____

## ACT 1
## Scene 2

*(The scene takes place in the woods. There are many small boulders and stones. Center stage is a large stone. Merlin walks onstage, looking in all directions to be certain no one is near. He walks to the stone and taps it on all sides with the sword. The purpose is to show the audience that the stone appears to be completely solid and unable to be moved from its location.)*

**Merlin:** This is the ideal stone. I shall lodge Excalibur in this stone, and Excalibur shall wait patiently for the rightful heir to pull it from its resting place.

*(Merlin holds Excalibur with one hand and waves his other hand over the stone as he hums in a monotone. Then he plunges Excalibur into the stone, all the way up to the handle.)*

**Merlin:** Excalibur, I lodge you in this stone as tightly as a key stuck in a rusty lock. Here, you will remain firm. None shall be able to pull you from your resting place—except Arthur, the rightful heir to the throne.

*(Merlin unrolls a paper that appears to be a proclamation and nails it to a tree near the stone.)*

**Merlin:** I shall post this notice for all to see. Whomsoever can pull this sword from the stone will be declared the king of England!

**FIGURATIVE LANGUAGE**
Circle the example of figurative language in Merlin's dialogue. What does this figurative language help you understand about Merlin and his intent?

_____

_____

_____

## ACT 2

*(The time is fifteen years later. Arthur is now fifteen years old. He sits in woods near the stone where Excalibur is lodged. A friend sits nearby. The two are concerned and are talking.)*

15 **Arthur:** Our country is in upheaval. We have no leader. We need a king, a ruler who will unite all our people.

**Randolph:** *(pointing to the sword in the stone)* It has been declared. There is only one rightful heir to the throne, and he shall be able to pull the sword from the stone. *(pauses)* You should try. Try to pull the sword from the stone.

**Arthur:** *(shaking his head and chuckling)* I'm a peasant, not the son of a king. Such an endeavor would be foolish.

*(Richard, Edward, and Walton enter. They are dressed in knight's garb. They are laughing and are horsing around.)*

**Richard:** Ah, so here is the renowned sword in the stone. Watch me, my companions! I am a brave knight, and I must be the heir to the throne! I shall do my utmost to pull the sword from the stone.

**Edward:** *(pointing to the sword in the stone)* Ah, you foolish knight! The kingdom is mine. *I* shall pull the sword from the stone.

20 **Walton:** *(racing with the other two knights to the stone)* You are *both* wrong. I shall be the one to implement the most effective strategy. And *I* shall pull the sword from the throne.

*(Richard, Edward, and Walton shove and jostle one another as they approach the stone. Each tries to pull the sword from the stone, but none is successful. As they are trying, Merlin enters in the background. After all three have tried so hard that they are exhausted and have fallen to the ground, Merlin speaks.)*

**Merlin:** *(with disdain)* Enough! Our kingdom is in turmoil. We need a king. We must repel the enemies who threaten our country and our lives. And you knights roughhouse in our countryside!

**Edward:** *(sheepishly)* We meant no disrespect. We have heard tales of the stone and the contentment and prosperity that could come to our country if the sword could be pulled out.

**Walton:** What will become of our land if the rightful heir does not come forward soon?

### ELEMENTS OF DRAMA
How much time has passed between Acts 1 and 2? What effect does this change in the setting have on the plot?

_____

_____

_____

### MAKE INFERENCES
What does Arthur's comment suggest about what might have happened during the time between Acts 1 and 2?

_____

_____

_____

### CHARACTERS  Why do the knights' attitudes change so suddenly?

_____

_____

_____

**MAKE INFERENCES**

Why does Merlin suggest that Arthur try to remove the sword from the stone instead of telling him that he is heir to the throne?

_____

_____

_____

**PLOT** What is the problem in the play? How is it resolved?

_____

_____

_____

**THEME** What is the theme of the play?

_____

_____

_____

**Richard:** Since the death of our esteemed King Uther, we have had no king. Our land has been filled with peril. And now enemies try to close us in from all sides. If the rightful heir is not soon discovered, we fear our country will fall to these enemies.

25 **Merlin:** *(looking directly at Arthur)* The time has come. The rightful heir must take the throne. All that remains is for the heir to pull Excalibur from the stone. Then the kingdom will be set right again.

**Arthur:** *(looking very confused)* Yes, Merlin, I agree. But what can I do?

*(In the background, there are sounds of enemy soldiers approaching from the distance. All characters tense up and look extremely apprehensive.)*

**Merlin:** *(gesturing toward the sword in the stone)* Try it, Arthur. Try to pull the sword from the stone. The sword will grant great power to the rightful heir. It will help to bring peace and prosperity to our country, so that all may have food and homes, so that peace will be able to return to our country once again. Now, hurry Arthur! We haven't much time.

*(Arthur approaches the stone, looking skeptical. He reaches to pull the sword, and it easily comes out of the stone. His demeanor immediately changes. He stands tall and confident, and he holds the sword up high, pointing it toward the sky. Spotlights shine on the sword. The noise of the approaching enemy soldiers begins to die away.)*

**Merlin:** *(gesturing toward the sword in the stone)* Excalibur is pulled from the stone. All hail King Arthur!

**All characters except Arthur:** *(bowing)* All hail the king!

*(Lights dim, and curtain falls.)*

## Anchor Standard Discussion Questions

Discuss the following questions with your peer group. Then record your answers in the space provided.

1. In Act 1, Merlin decides that Arthur should be raised as a "peasant child." How do you think Arthur's peasant upbringing might have shaped his character? Do you think this background will help Arthur as king? Support your answer with details from the text.

_____

_____

_____

_____

_____

_____

2. Reread the following stage directions from near the end of the Act 2.

   *(Arthur approaches the stone, looking skeptical. He reaches to pull the sword, and it easily comes out of the stone. His demeanor immediately changes. He stands tall and confident, and he holds the sword up high, pointing it toward the sky. Spotlights shine on the sword. The noise of the approaching enemy soldiers begins to die away.)*

   What is the significance of these stage directions? What do they suggest about Arthur and the future of the kingdom? Support your answer with details from the text.

_____

_____

_____

_____

_____

## Comprehension Check

1. How might the plot be different if Arthur knew as a child that he was the heir to the kingdom?

_____

_____

_____

2. How do the ways in which Merlin honors his promise to King Uther show how Merlin feels about Arthur?

_____

_____

_____

3. How is Merlin able to ensure that only Arthur would possess Excalibur?

_____

_____

_____

## Read On Your Own

Read another drama, "Things That Go Bump in the Day," independently. Apply what you learned in this lesson and check your understanding.

# Reading Scientific and Technical Texts

**Look at this** view of Earth from space.

Have you ever wondered what lies under the surface of the land and water?

**ESSENTIAL QUESTION**

*How does visual information help the reader to understand scientific and technical texts?*

**Consider ▶** What text structures are often used in scientific and technical texts?

How do graphics, symbols, and scientific terms clarify scientific and technical texts?

# Journey to
# EARTH'S CENTER

1    Considering a journey to Earth's center brings to mind all sorts of wild, awe-inspiring feats. So it was with Jules Verne and his book *Journey to the Center of the Earth*. Today, though, we know that the story Verne wrote describes a journey into pure fantasy. The high pressure and temperature in Earth's core make it impossible for humans to survive there.

Now, you might ask yourself: *If humans couldn't survive deep in Earth's interior, how do we know so much about the interior layers?* Your question would certainly be valid. Geologists study rocks and other physical features of planet Earth as well as its history. Geophysicists study the relationship between Earth's features and the forces that change or produce them. These scientists have learned about the planet's interior from experiments with Earth's rocks and minerals and from the data gained through studies of earthquake waves. In laboratories, scientists apply extreme heat and pressure to rocks and minerals to learn more about the ways heat and pressure within Earth affect them. In the field, scientists study the vibrations produced by earthquakes. The speed at which these vibrations travel offers clues about the rocks through which they are traveling. Scientists' understanding of earthquake data grows deeper as time passes.

Scientists have learned that Earth is divided into layers called the crust, mantle, and core, based on composition. Each layer is significantly hotter and under greater pressure than the one above it.

**ANALYZE SCIENTIFIC TEXTS** Scientific texts provide facts about living things, nonliving things, Earth and space, and physical properties. Why can this passage be accurately identified as scientific text?

## The Crust

Earth's crust, being the outermost layer, is the easiest to study. The crust is a layer of light, solid rock. Most of the crust is made up of eight elements: oxygen (O), silicon (Si), aluminum (Al), iron (Fe), calcium (Ca), sodium (Na), potassium (K), and magnesium (Mg). It makes sense that scientists have gained the greatest knowledge about this layer. Ocean basins and the ground beneath your feet are part of Earth's crust. Think of Earth's crust the way you think about crust on a piece of bread. This will help you visualize that the crust is quite thin—at least in comparison to Earth's deeper layers. The oceanic crust, the crust beneath the oceans, is much thinner than the continental crust, which makes up the continents.

## The Mantle

5      Below the crust is the mantle. The mantle is much hotter and softer than the crust, and it makes up most of Earth's volume. The part of the mantle closest to the crust, called the upper mantle, is solid and fractures easily. At greater depths, the temperature and pressure rise in a region called the lower mantle. This causes rock to flow like a slow-moving liquid. The rock is not actually melted, but it is hot enough to fold, stretch, compress, and slowly flow without fracturing. Because of heat and pressure, the rock within the inner mantle is less rigid than the rock above and below. It flows at a slow pace, the way in which gooey, sticky clay might move. This flexibility allows the upper mantle and crust above it to move.

**SCIENCE SYMBOLS** Scientists often use symbols for elements. Why do you think the author has included both the written names and symbols for the elements that make up Earth's crust?

**SCIENCE TERMS** A science term is a word or phrase found in a scientific text. What are the component parts of the mantle?

**AUTHOR'S PURPOSE** The author's purpose is the reason for writing: to entertain, to inform, to persuade, or to express. What is most likely the author's main purpose for writing this passage? Explain.

## The Core

Earth's core is made up of the outer core and the inner core. The outer core is molten, which means that it has been turned to liquid by extreme heat. This core is made of hot liquid iron and nickel. Scientists think that the outer core is instrumental in the control of Earth's magnetic field, as this liquid metal portion of the core spins while Earth rotates.

The inner core is solid and is made almost completely of extremely hot iron. It is acted on by the extreme pressure of all the layers above it. To get a sense of the extraordinary heat at the center of Earth's core, think about this fact: it is hotter than the sun's surface!

### Earth's Magnetic Field

North Magnetic Pole

South Magnetic Pole

Scientists think that the liquid iron in Earth's core produces the planet's magnetic field.

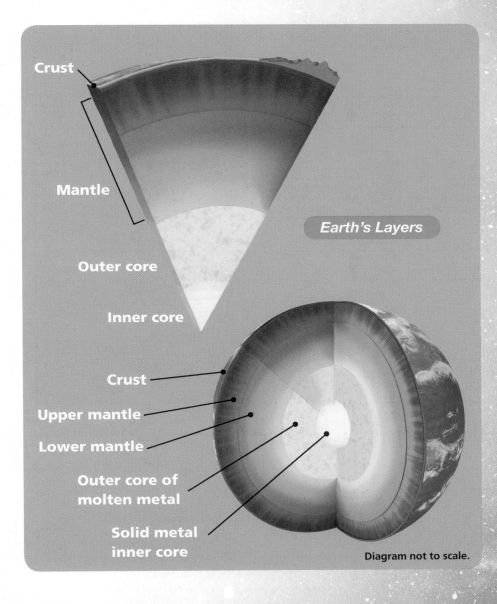

Crust

Mantle

Outer core

Inner core

*Earth's Layers*

Crust

Upper mantle

Lower mantle

Outer core of molten metal

Solid metal inner core

Diagram not to scale.

**ANALYZE SCIENTIFIC TEXTS** You can use definitions, context, and graphics to help you understand scientific texts. Which of Earth's layers is directly beneath your feet? How can you tell?

**GRAPHICS** A diagram delivers information in a visual way. What is Earth's outermost layer? How does the diagram help you understand this?

## Comprehension Check

Think about someone digging from Earth's crust to its inner core. List in order the layers through which the person would travel, and give a brief description of each layer. Use information from "Journey to Earth's Center" to help you.

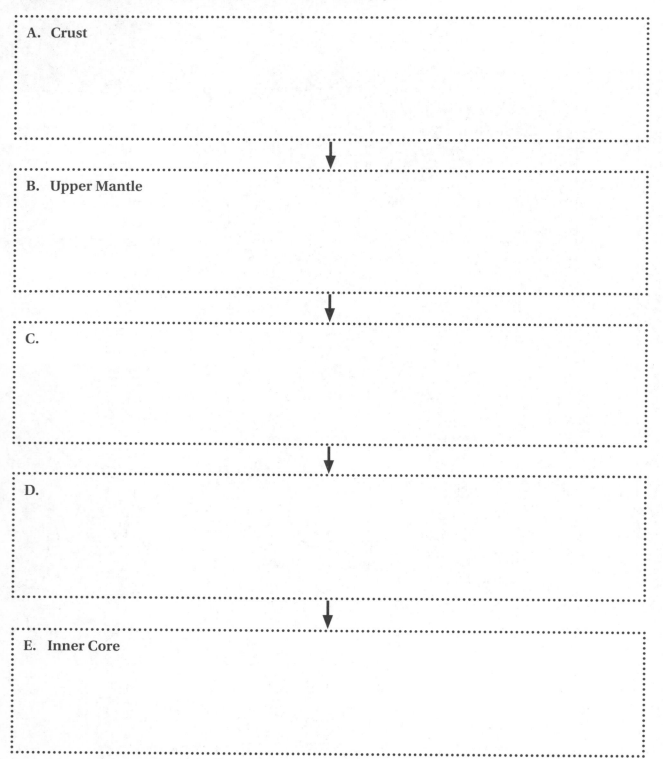

A.  Crust

B.  Upper Mantle

C.

D.

E.  Inner Core

## Vocabulary

Use the word map below to help you define and use one of the highlighted vocabulary words from the Share and Learn selection you are about to read or another word you choose.

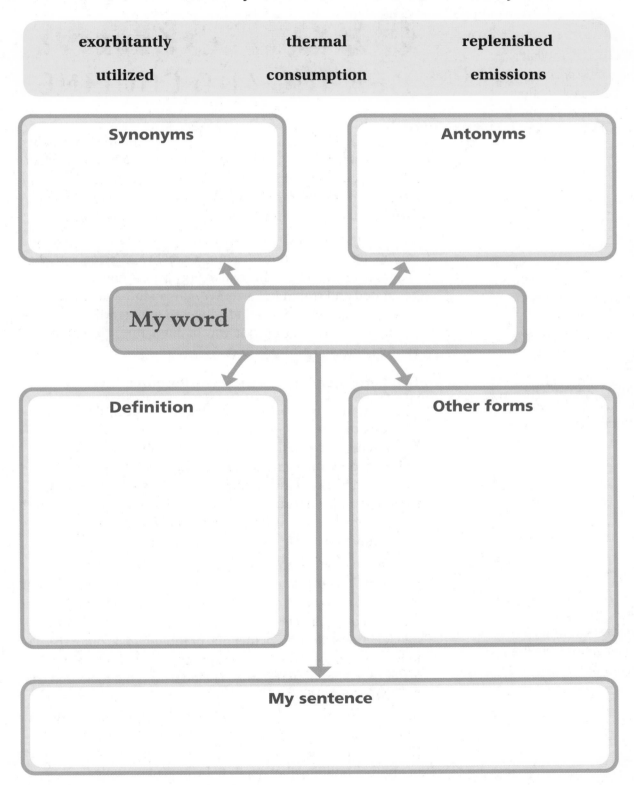

| exorbitantly | thermal | replenished |
| utilized | consumption | emissions |

**Synonyms**

**Antonyms**

**My word**

**Definition**

**Other forms**

**My sentence**

**Consider ▶** Why is it important to use renewable resources for energy?

How can we use heat from Earth's interior to heat our homes?

# Geothermal
## HEATING AND COOLING

**CONTEXT CLUES** What does the word *convert* mean in paragraph 2? How do context clues help you figure out the meaning?

_____

_____

_____

**CENTRAL IDEA** Circle the paragraph that includes the best statement of the central idea of the passage.

**SUMMARY** How would you summarize what you have read in paragraph 3?

_____

_____

_____

**ROOTS AND AFFIXES** In the word *geothermal*, what does *geo* mean? What other words start with *geo*? What other words have the root *therm*?

_____

_____

_____

1    Energy! It's become so much a part of "fueling" our daily lives. Sometimes we don't think enough about how it reaches us. Of course, that can change when we see an oil refinery spewing flames and smoke into the air—or when a family receives an exorbitantly high energy bill for heat or air conditioning.

Is it just a dream to think we could harness energy while producing less pollution? It's not! It's reality. Thermal energy is heat energy, and geothermal energy is heat energy that is generated and stored in Earth. We can tap into Earth's interior to access this heat energy and convert it into a form we can use, such as electrical power. One way of doing this is by using a geothermal heat pump system.

**Geothermal Energy: A Renewable Resource**

Nonrenewable resources such as oil, coal, and natural gas will run out. They require thousands or millions of years to form, but humans can use them in the blink of an eye, much more quickly than nature can replace them. Renewable resources, though, can be replenished by nature within a much shorter period of time. For example, when you consider the water cycle, you can observe that water is a renewable resource. It is constantly moving through the water cycle.

Take a moment to think about the parts of the word *geothermal*. These word parts help to make its meaning clear. But where exactly is geothermal energy accessed? Some of this energy is accessed within feet of Earth's surface, and some requires deeper access. Pockets of magma, or molten rock, often rise close to Earth's surface. The magma transfers heat to rocks, as well as to water that flows underground. The heat from the rocks and water is utilized by geothermal power plants—as well as homes and office buildings—to produce electricity. To produce this electricity, a heat pump, or heat exchanger, moves thermal energy from Earth's interior into a geothermal power plant, a specific home, or another building that needs to be heated or cooled.

### Geothermal Power Plants: Energy Conversion

5     The U.S. Environmental Protection Agency (EPA) states that geothermal heat pumps can have a significant impact on our environment by substantially reducing nonrenewable energy consumption and the emissions they produce. Geothermal energy is one of the least expensive renewable energy sources we can use every day.

    Geothermal heat pump systems can both cool and heat. They require 25 to 50 percent less electricity than the types of heating and cooling systems most people have in their homes. Most families with heat pump systems spend about 75 percent less on their heating and cooling bills than families who live in homes without them.

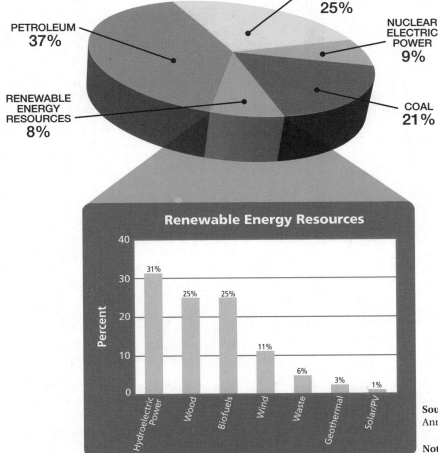

**Primary Energy Consumption in the United States by Source: 2010**

NATURAL GAS 25%
NUCLEAR ELECTRIC POWER 9%
PETROLEUM 37%
RENEWABLE ENERGY RESOURCES 8%
COAL 21%

**Renewable Energy Resources**

Percent (0, 10, 20, 30, 40)

- Hydroelectric Power 31%
- Wood 25%
- Biofuels 25%
- Wind 11%
- Waste 6%
- Geothermal 3%
- Solar/PV 1%

**Source:** U.S. Energy Information Administration Annual Energy Review, 2010

**Note:** Percentages are rounded.

**ANALYZE SCIENTIFIC AND TECHNICAL TEXTS** What is the EPA? How can you tell? Why is the EPA's statement about geothermal heating and cooling important?

_____

_____

**USE REFERENCE SOURCES** What reference source could you use to find a synonym for the word *impact*? What would an effective synonym be?

_____

_____

**GRAPHICS** Which portion of the circle graph is expanded on in the bar graph below it? Which type of energy was consumed the least in the United States during this time? Given the information in the graph and in paragraph 5, why might the EPA want to promote the use of geothermal energy?

_____

_____

## AUTHOR'S PURPOSE
What is most likely the author's main purpose for writing this passage? Explain.

_____

_____

_____

## GRAPHICS How does the time line help you understand geothermal energy use?

_____

_____

_____

## SCIENCE TERMS The time line mentions the term *greenhouse gases*. What are greenhouse gases?

_____

_____

_____

## TEXT STRUCTURE What is the text structure of the time line? Explain.

_____

_____

_____

## Geothermal Energy Use: Not as New as You Might Think

While you might think that using geothermal energy is relatively new, it's been around for thousands of years. Scientific discoveries have revealed that Paleo-Indians in North America utilized hot springs (natural flows of hot water that have come to Earth's surface) more than ten thousand years ago for a variety of purposes, including heating and bathing. Of course, our knowledge and use of geothermal energy have come a long way since then. Take a look at the time line below to learn more about the journey.

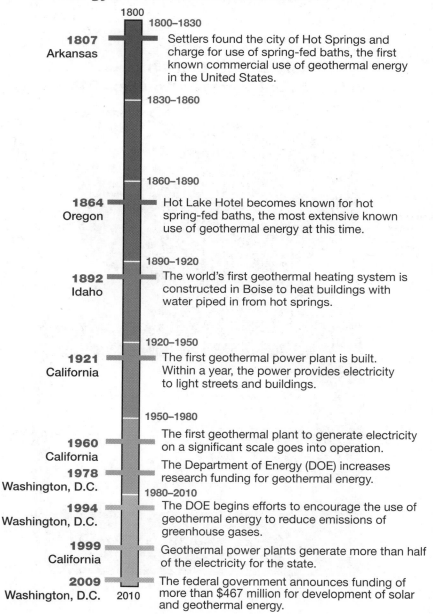

### Significant Events in Geothermal Energy Use Across the United States

1800

**1800–1830**

**1807 Arkansas** — Settlers found the city of Hot Springs and charge for use of spring-fed baths, the first known commercial use of geothermal energy in the United States.

**1830–1860**

**1860–1890**

**1864 Oregon** — Hot Lake Hotel becomes known for hot spring-fed baths, the most extensive known use of geothermal energy at this time.

**1890–1920**

**1892 Idaho** — The world's first geothermal heating system is constructed in Boise to heat buildings with water piped in from hot springs.

**1920–1950**

**1921 California** — The first geothermal power plant is built. Within a year, the power provides electricity to light streets and buildings.

**1950–1980**

**1960 California** — The first geothermal plant to generate electricity on a significant scale goes into operation.

**1978 Washington, D.C.** — The Department of Energy (DOE) increases research funding for geothermal energy.

**1980–2010**

**1994 Washington, D.C.** — The DOE begins efforts to encourage the use of geothermal energy to reduce emissions of greenhouse gases.

**1999 California** — Geothermal power plants generate more than half of the electricity for the state.

**2009 Washington, D.C.** 2010 — The federal government announces funding of more than $467 million for development of solar and geothermal energy.

## Anchor Standard Discussion Question

**Discuss the following question with your peer group. Then record your answers in the space provided.**

1. California utilizes about two-thirds of the United States' geothermal power. What makes California particularly suitable for harnessing geothermal power? Why do you think less geothermal energy is harnessed in other states, such as North Dakota or Wisconsin? Support your answer with details from "Geothermal Heating and Cooling" as well as what you learned about Earth's layers in "Journey to Earth's Center."

## Comprehension Check

1. Why it is important to understand the scientific terms and technical meanings in the passage?

_____

_____

_____

2. Write a summary of the passage "Geothermal Heating and Cooling."

_____

_____

_____

3. What are the benefits of using geothermal energy as opposed to using refined oil for heating purposes?

_____

_____

_____

### Read On Your Own

Read another scientific and technical text, "Arctic Survival," independently. Apply what you learned in this lesson and check your understanding.

# Writing Informative Texts

## ESSENTIAL QUESTION

*How do informative texts use facts and details to explain or deliver information effectively?*

**Each year** people travel all over the world to see new places, experience different cultures, and engage in leisure activities. Some vacationers visit historical sites. They enjoy imagining life in different times and learning about events and people from the distant past. You may have visited an interesting historical site. You may have read plaques, brochures, or other information about the place before, during, or after your trip. How would you tell someone about what you saw, learned, and experienced? One way would be to write an informative text.

# What's an Informative Text?

Historians and social scientists sometimes write about places where cultures and civilizations have developed or thrived and then disappeared. They must do a lot of research before they even begin writing. They use their research to find facts, details, examples, and quotations.

In an **informative text**, you provide information or explain something about a topic. You state your topic and develop it using facts, details, examples, explanations, and quotations. Read the ways to present information effectively in writing.

**Introductory Sentence**
Capture your readers' attention with a question, an interesting fact, or a story to draw the readers into the topic.

**Sentence Introducing Topic**
State the main idea you want readers to understand about the topic. The statement should explain to readers what you plan to inform them about.

**Evidence of Facts, Details, Examples, and Quotations**
Support your topic sentence with facts, details, examples, and quotations drawn from research. The more interesting they are, the stronger your writing will be.

**Conclusion**
Make a final statement that summarizes or restates your topic sentence.

Let's look at an informative text.

## Analyze a Mentor Text

This is an example of an effective informative text by a sixth grader. Read it and then complete the activities in the boxes as a class.

### The Ancient City of Tikal

Imagine that you leave a large city at dawn on a bus that travels north through the rain forest. Then you walk along a jungle path where howler monkeys screech from the trees. Toucans, cockatoos, and other birds call out from the 100-foot canopy of the forest. Finally, as you near the top of a winding trail, you see the ruins of a city open up before you. The ancient city of Tikal is a treasure because it gives people an idea of what Mayan civilization might have been like.

When the Mayan center of Tikal was discovered in 1848, archaeologists—social scientists who study people and cultures from the past—found more than they had ever imagined. They realized that a mighty city lay buried beneath the layers of jungle growth. It had been deserted for hundreds of years. Tikal was a large city even by today's standards. The site covers 50 square miles. It contains the ruins of more than 3,000 buildings, including temples, pyramids, palaces, and houses. As many as 400,000 people may have lived there at one time. Tikal reached the height of its power between 1,200 and 1,700 years ago. However, the Maya may have started building on the site as early as 2,600 years ago.

**INTRODUCE THE TOPIC**
The writer includes a sentence about Tikal in paragraph 1 to inform readers of what they will be reading about. Draw a box around the sentence that introduces the topic.

**FACTS, DETAILS, AND EXAMPLES** The writer develops the topic by providing facts and details about the ancient city of Tikal, including background about the city as well as a vivid description of what it looked like long ago. Underline two facts or details paragraph 2.

**FACTS, DETAILS, AND EXAMPLES** The writer continues to develop the topic by providing facts, details, and examples about what the ancient city of Tikal teaches us about Mayan life and civilization. What is one example given in paragraph 4, and what does it illustrate about ancient Mayan life?

**CONCLUSION** The purpose of a conclusion is to summarize or restate the topic and include some final thoughts or ideas about it. Draw a box around the concluding statement in the last paragraph.

The Great Plaza, once the center of public life in Tikal, was surrounded by important structures. Today the Great Plaza is a giant rectangle covered with grass. Long ago, the plaza was paved with limestone plaster, as were the streets of Tikal. Along the short sides of the plaza sit two great pyramids. Farther up is the Temple of the Masks. From that spot, visitors can see west across the treetops to the building known as Temple IV, which rises 212 feet high. Temple IV was not only the biggest building in Tikal, it was also the tallest building in North and Central America until the 1800s. Altars and tall stone monuments called stelae dot the Great Plaza between the two pyramids.

Tikal also has several ball courts. Here, the Maya played a game called pok-ta-pok. Teams of men wore protective padding as they played with a solid rubber ball. Winners received great riches, while members of the losing team might sometimes face a death sentence!

Tikal was a busy place in ancient times. Giant roadways led into Tikal from miles around. On Mayan holidays, nobles wearing fine clothes and jewelry flocked into town from their estates. Farmers abandoned their fields in the jungle. Merchants arrived with their wares. Visitors came from other Mayan cities. Everyone came to celebrate, to watch pok-ta-pok, and to take part in religious rituals.

Tikal's glory days may be long gone, but the ancient city is still a wonderful place to learn about a thriving civilization from the past. Today, tourists from all over the world praise the achievements of the Maya, just as visitors did in ancient times.

**Think About It ▶** What is the most important idea the writer is trying to convey in this informative text?

Does the writer inform the reader using strong facts, details, and examples?

## Vocabulary Study: Academic Vocabulary

Informative texts, such as "The Ancient City of Tikal," often include vocabulary words that you will encounter in social studies. Understanding these words will make you a better reader and writer. Words may be defined in the text or understood by using context clues. You may need to consult a dictionary to find their meanings.

Look at these academic vocabulary words, highlighted in the mentor text. Work with your class or a partner to complete this chart, using context clues and/or a dictionary.

| Academic Vocabulary | Meaning |
|---|---|
| rain forest | tropical woodland with high annual rainfall and tall trees whose tops form a continuous layer |
| ruins | |
| archaeologists | |

Now look at the mentor text on pages 119–120. Find three other highlighted words, and complete the chart below. Use context clues or a dictionary to figure out their meanings.

**Word**

**Meaning**

**Word**

**Meaning**

**Word**

**Meaning**

# Writing Process

Now that you have read and analyzed an informative text, you are going to create your own by following the steps of the writing process.

**1. Get Ready: Take Notes on Research** Select and evaluate the research resources you will use to investigate your topic. Consider whether the sources and information are reliable and accurate. Take notes on note cards as you read your resources. Cite the sources where you found the information in case you need to revisit the information as you write and so you can credit them. Look for information that best supports the topic. Keep a record of your sources.

**2. Organize** Use a graphic organizer to organize supporting facts, details, and examples and to plan your informative text.

**3. Draft** Create the first draft of your informative text. Make sure to state your topic clearly; develop it with facts, details, and examples; and provide a conclusion.

**4. Peer Review** Work with a partner to evaluate and improve your draft.

**5. Revise** Use suggestions from your peer review to revise your informative text.

**6. Edit** Check your work carefully for errors in spelling, punctuation, and grammar.

**7. Publish** Create a final version of your informative text.

## Writing Assignment

In this chapter, you will write your own informative text. As you create this text, remember the elements of the mentor text that were most effective. Read the following assignment.

> The city of Pompeii in Italy is a site of ancient ruins. The city was partially buried by a volcanic eruption in 79 CE. Write at least five paragraphs describing Pompeii and its features. The text should include details from research texts and a conclusion.

# 1. Get Ready: Take Notes on Research

The writer of the mentor text wrote about the ancient city of Tikal. Before she could write a draft, she researched her topic. Here is a paragraph from one of the articles she found.

> For many centuries, the lost site of Tikal lay hidden in the jungle. It had been abandoned for unknown reasons over 1,000 years before. Among the natives, there was a legend of a lost city. But nobody had ever seen such a place in various explorations. Finally, in 1848, the mystery was solved when a man by the name of Ambrosio Tut discovered Tikal. Soon, curious experts were traveling from all over the world to explore the findings.

The writer took notes on each of the articles she found. Here is the note card that she filled out for the text above. What kinds of information does she include?

| |
|---|
| **Important Idea:** For many centuries, the lost site of Tikal lay hidden in the jungle. |
| **Detail:** Tikal had been abandoned for unknown reasons 1,000 years before. |
| **Detail:** Natives told a legend of a lost city. |
| **Detail:** Ambrosio Tut discovered Tikal in 1848. |
| **Detail:** Experts soon came from all over to see it. |
| **Source:** *The Great City of Tikal* by Amber Greene. Philadelphia: Goldhaven Press, 1993. |

**IMPORTANT IDEA** The writer listed an important idea from the passage to include in her informative text. Underline it.

**DETAILS** The writer listed notes about details from the passage, such as "Natives told a legend of a lost city." Circle the detail you find most interesting.

**SOURCE** Finally, the writer gave the source for the passage so that she can give credit to the source's author. Draw two lines under the source.

## Researching Text

Your topic is the ancient city of Pompeii. Here is some information that you might use in your informative text. Read the text. Think about the important, or main, ideas in each paragraph. Also think about interesting details that you might want to use in your informative piece.

**DETAILS** Paragraph 1 introduces the volcano and the ancient city. Which details do you find most interesting in the paragraph?

**IMPORTANT IDEA/ DETAILS** Underline the most important idea in paragraph 2. Which interesting details would you use in your informative piece?

**QUOTATION** Why might the quotation be effective to use in your informative piece?

*from*
# The Secrets of Pompeii
*by Jennifer Woodson*

In 79 CE, the great volcano Mount Vesuvius erupted, burying the city of Pompeii for almost 1,700 years. Not until 1748 did archaeologists begin to uncover the ancient city. What they found amazed them. Buried beneath volcanic ash was a wealthy Roman town frozen in time, full of artifacts that showed the world what life had been like right before the eruption.

Mount Vesuvius had not blown its top in more than 1,500 years, so the people of Pompeii had no idea that it was going to erupt. When it started, the violent eruption lasted twenty-four hours. Pliny the Younger, a Roman who witnessed the event from a distance, wrote that "Darkness fell, not the dark of a moonless or cloudy night, but as if the lamp had been put out in a dark room."

# Try It!

**Record Your Notes**

Use these note cards to take notes on the text about Pompeii. Remember, write the main ideas, interesting details, and a quotation that you want to use for each paragraph. Finally, give the source of the information.

**Important Idea:**

**Detail:**

**Detail:**

**Detail:**

**Source:**

**Important Idea:**

**Detail:**

**Detail:**

**Quotation:**

**Source:**

## Researching Text, *continued*

Here is more information you might use in your informative text. Read the articles, and take notes on relevant details.

**RELEVANCE**
Relevant details are the ones that are directly connected to your main idea. Which of the facts in this source are *not* relevant to your topic? Draw a line through them.

*from*
# The Encyclopedia of Ancient Civilizations
*by Marc Williams*

Before Mount Vesuvius erupted, the city of Pompeii was a wealthy port city, well known for its trade. As many as 20,000 people lived there. The streets were laid out in a grid. Citizens held a wide variety of jobs, from merchants to farmers to slaves. Many of the well-to-do citizens had sophisticated homes. Hot air was used to heat the homes, and some even had running water that traveled through aqueducts from the city's reservoir. The aqueducts also fed swimming pools for public bathing and other public water sources. The city had additional infrastructure, as well. A public outdoor theater, called an amphitheatre, provided a place for local citizens to gather for entertainment. People could exercise and socialize at the public gymnasium. Food markets and small restaurants dotted the city. Today, Pompeii is a popular tourist destination.

**CREDIBILITY**
Credible sources are believable ones. This source comes from an individual's blog. What language from this source makes you suspect its credibility? Circle the words or phrases that harm the source's credibility.

# My Travel Blog

Last year, I visited Pompeii to see what the ancient ruins looked like. What a cool place! It is much larger than I imagined from my reading in history classes. As I walked about the archaeological site, I could picture what the town must have been like long ago. I could see some of the buildings that have been partly restored and picture cute kids running in and out of them. I saw plaster casts of the voids left by the dead bodies. That was a little freaky! Some of the famous frescoes are on display, and I stood there with my mouth open in awe as I looked at them. From the town, I could see Mount Vesuvius in the distance. It's about 8 miles away from the town that it completely destroyed so long ago. It's so awe-inspiring that such a great tragedy ended up preserving life exactly as it was happening. I am so lucky that I got to see all these beautiful relics.

# Try It!

**Record Your Notes**

Use these note cards to take notes on the texts about Pompeii. Remember, write the main ideas and interesting details that you want to use for each paragraph. Finally, give the source of the information.

| **Important Idea:** |
| --- |
| **Detail:** |
| **Detail:** |
| **Detail:** |
| **Source:** |

| **Important Idea:** |
| --- |
| **Detail:** |
| **Detail:** |
| **Detail:** |
| **Source:** |

## Researching Visual Information

When you research a topic, you will discover that information can be provided in different ways. You may find photographs, charts, tables, or diagrams in books or in online resources. Charts, graphs, and tables can also be used in an informative piece to organize information and ideas. You can use note cards to record notes about these different forms of information, too.

The first example shows a photograph and a painting. The second example shows a time line. Think about how you could use these graphics to find ideas and details about Pompeii.

**Ruins of Pompeii, with Mount Vesuvius in the background**

**INFORMATION IN ART** How could you use the information shown in the photograph and the painting to help you describe what happened in Pompeii in 79 CE?

**Johan Christian Clausen Dahl, *Outbreak of the Vesuvius* (1826)**

**INFORMATION IN TIME LINE** How could this time line help you write about the sequence of events in your informative text about Pompeii? What information would you use?

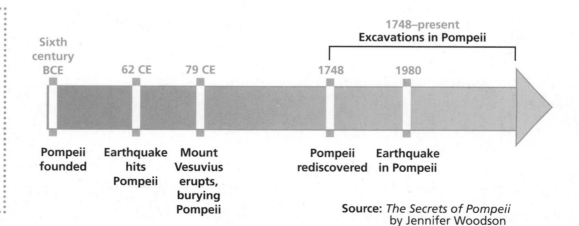

**Source:** *The Secrets of Pompeii* by Jennifer Woodson

# Try It!  **Record Your Notes**

Use these note cards to take notes on the photograph, painting, and time line shown on the previous page. You can use your answers from the activities on that page to help you.

| Important Idea (Photograph and Painting): |
| :--- |
| **Detail:** |
| **Detail:** |
| **Detail:** |
| **Source:** |

| Important Idea (Time Line): |
| :--- |
| **Detail:** |
| **Detail:** |
| **Detail:** |
| **Source:** |

# 2. Organize

You are almost ready to begin a draft of your informative text. You can use a graphic organizer to help show and order the facts, details, and examples that you gathered during your research. You can then refer to the graphic organizer as you work through the different parts of your draft. The writer of the mentor text completed this graphic organizer.

**INTRODUCTION**
In the first paragraph, introduce the topic of your informative text.

**SUPPORTING PARAGRAPHS**
In subsequent paragraphs, give evidence that develops your topic, such as facts, details, examples, and quotations.

**CONCLUSION**
In the final paragraph, restate the topic and summarize your main ideas. Also provide some final thoughts.

**Topic Sentence**
The ancient city of Tikal is a treasure because it gives people an idea of what Mayan civilization might have been like.

**Idea 1** When the city of Tikal was discovered in 1848, archaeologists realized it had been a mighty city.
**Supporting facts, examples, or details:**
- site measures 50 square miles
- 3,000 buildings: temples, pyramids, palaces, houses
- as many as 400,000 inhabitants

**Idea 2** The Great Plaza was the center of public life and was surrounded by important structures.
**Supporting facts, examples, or details:**
- plaza paved with limestone plaster
- two great pyramids on the short sides
- altars and tall stone monuments

**Idea 3** Tikal had ball courts.
**Supporting facts, examples, or details:**
- played pok-ta-pok with rubber ball
- protective padding for players
- winners richly rewarded, losers sentenced to death

**Idea 4** Tikal was a thriving center.
**Supporting facts, examples, or details:**
- giant roadways that led into Tikal from surrounding areas
- gathering place for Mayan holidays

**Conclusion**
Tikal's glory days may be gone, but the ancient city is still a wonderful place to learn about a past civilization. Tourists from all over the world visit Tikal.

# Try It!

**Organize Your Informative Text**

Now use the graphic organizer below to organize the supporting facts, details, examples, and quotations.

**Topic sentence**

**Idea 1**
**Supporting facts, details, examples, or quotations:**

**Idea 2**
**Supporting facts, details, examples, or quotations:**

**Idea 3**
**Supporting facts, details, examples, or quotations:**

**Idea 4**
**Supporting facts, details, examples, or quotations:**

**Conclusion**

# 3. Draft

Now it is time to write the first draft of your informative text. Remember that a draft is just a draft; it is not the final product. Use your notes, jot down your ideas in an organized way, and experiment with different ways to convey your research. You will have time to revise your writing later. Start by drafting your informative text on a computer or on a separate sheet of paper. State your topic. Then develop it using facts, details, examples and quotations.

## Writer's Craft: Transition Words and Phrases

Writers use transition words and phrases to connect ideas within a piece of writing. They use them as signals to the readers to help them understand that the writing is moving from one idea to another idea. In informative writing, transitions can help readers understand time order, cause-and-effect relationships, and comparisons and contrasts. Look at the words below, which send a signal to the readers that a transition is being made from one idea to the next.

| | |
|---|---|
| **time order** | first, then, next, after, later, while, finally, during, soon, eventually |
| **cause and effect** | so, if, then, since, because, therefore, as a result, for this reason, consequently |
| **compare and contrast** | similar, different, on the other hand, but, however, in the same way, bigger than, smaller than, like, while |

The writer of the mentor text uses transition words and phrases. Underline the transition words and phrases in the paragraph that follows:

**TRANSITION WORDS AND PHRASES** Underline the transition words that show time order. Circle the transition word that shows a cause-and-effect relationship.

Imagine that you leave a large city at dawn on a bus that travels north through the rain forest. Then you walk along a jungle path where howler monkeys screech from the trees. Toucans, cockatoos, and other birds call out from the 100-foot canopy of the forest. Finally, as you near the top of a winding trail, you see the ruins of a city open up before you. The ancient city of Tikal is a treasure because it gives people an idea of what Mayan civilization might have been like.

# Try It! Write Your First Draft

On a computer or a separate sheet of paper, create the draft of your informative text. Remember to use words, phrases, and clauses that show clear relationships among ideas in your piece. Use this drafting checklist to help you as you write.

✓ A good introduction draws readers in and gets their attention. You can begin with a question, a quotation, a statement that the reader can relate to, or an interesting or funny experience.

✓ Be sure to state your topic in the first paragraph.

✓ Use the supporting facts, details, and examples you researched during Step 2: Organize.

✓ In each supporting paragraph, include sentences with details, facts, and examples.

✓ Cite the sources for any quotations correctly.

✓ Restate your topic and summarize your main ideas in the conclusion. Try adding something for your readers to think about in the future.

## Tips for Writing Your First Draft

- Talk to others about your topic. These discussions may lead you to new information that should be included in your draft.
- Write down key phrases and ideas before you begin writing. Sometimes this is a great warm-up to get you started.
- Write each supporting paragraph on an index card first. This makes it easier to move paragraphs around to determine the best order for your supporting ideas.
- Use transition words to guide the reader through the text, from one idea to the next.

# 4. Peer Review

After you finish your draft, you can work with a partner to review each other's drafts. Here is a draft of the mentor text. Read it with your partner. Together, answer the questions in the boxes. Then we'll see how the writer's classmate evaluated the draft.

**INTRODUCTION**
In the draft, the writer does not state the topic clearly. Compare the sentence with the one in the mentor text.

**SUPPORTING PARAGRAPHS**
Supporting paragraphs 2 and 3 could use more details and examples to develop the main idea in each. What details can be added to paragraph 2? What examples can be added to paragraph 3?

**CONCLUSION** This conclusion does not restate the topic clearly, but it does explain that people visit Tikal today. How would you improve the conclusion?

## The Ancient City of Tikal

Imagine that you leave a large city at dawn on a bus that travels north through the rain forest. Then you walk along a jungle path where howler monkeys screech from the trees. Toucans, cockatoos, and other birds call out from the 100-foot canopy of the forest. Finally, as you near the top of a winding trail, you see the ruins of a city open up before you. It is the ancient Mayan city of Tikal and it is a treasure.

When the Mayan center of Tikal was discovered in 1848, scientists realized that a mighty city lay buried beneath the layers. It had been deserted for hundreds of years. Tikal was a large city even by today's standards. A lot of people probably lived there. Tikal reached the height of its power between 1,200 and 1,700 years ago. However, the Maya may have started building there as early as 2,600 years ago.

The Great Plaza, once the center of public life in Tikal, was surrounded by important structures. Today the Great Plaza is a giant rectangle covered with grass. Long ago, the plaza was paved with limestone plaster. Visitors can see west across the treetops to a building known as Temple IV, which was the tallest building in North and Central America until the 1800s.

Today, tourists from all over the world come to visit Tikal. They praise the achievements of the Maya, just as visitors did in ancient times.

# An Example Peer Review Form

This peer review form gives an example of how a classmate evaluated the draft of the mentor text shown on the previous page.

| | |
|---|---|
| **The introduction begins in an interesting way.**<br><br>**The writer states the topic clearly.** | You did a good job of making the beginning interesting. |
| | You could improve your informative text by introducing the topic more clearly. |

| | |
|---|---|
| **The writer supports the topic sentence with at least three strong facts, details, examples, or quotations.**<br><br>**The writer uses interesting facts, details, examples, or quotations to support the topic sentence.** | You did a good job of giving more than three facts, details, or examples. |
| | You could improve your informative text by adding facts, details, examples, or quotations to each paragraph to support your topic sentence. |

| | |
|---|---|
| **The writer uses words, clauses, and phrases to make the writing flow smoothly and to connect ideas.** | You did a good job of using the transition "however" in paragraph 2 to show contrast. |
| | You could improve your informative text by adding more transition words. |

| | |
|---|---|
| **The writer restates the topic.**<br><br>**The conclusion leaves the reader with a few interesting details or ideas to think about.** | You did a good job of restating the importance of Tikal. |
| | You could improve your informative text by adding an interesting detail or idea for the reader to think about. |

# Try It!

**Peer Review with a Partner**

Now you are going to work with a partner to review each other's informative text drafts. You will use the peer review form below. If you need help, look back at the mentor text writer's peer review form for suggestions.

| | |
|---|---|
| **The introduction begins in an interesting way.**<br><br>**The writer states the topic clearly.** | You did a good job of<br><br>You could improve your informative text by |
| **The writer develops the topic with at least three strong facts, details, examples, or quotations.**<br><br>**The writer uses interesting facts, details, examples, or quotations to develop the topic.** | You did a good job of<br><br>You could improve your informative text by |
| **The writer uses words, clauses, and phrases to make the writing flow smoothly and to connect ideas.** | You did a good job of<br><br>You could improve your informative text by |
| **The writer restates the topic.**<br><br>**The conclusion leaves the reader with a few interesting details or ideas to think about.** | You did a good job of<br><br>You could improve your informative text by |

# Try It!

**Record Key Peer Review Comments**

Now it is time for you and your partner to share your comments with each other. Listen to your partner's feedback, and write down the key comments that you hear in the left column. Then write some ideas for improving your draft in the right column.

| | |
|---|---|
| My review says that my introduction | I will |
| My review says that my topic is stated | I will |
| My review says that my first supporting fact, detail, example, or quotation | I will |
| My review says that my second supporting fact, detail, example, or quotation | I will |
| My review says that my third supporting fact, detail, example, or quotation | I will |
| My review says that my fourth supporting fact, detail, example, or quotation | I will |
| My review says that my conclusion | I will |

Use the space below to write anything additional you notice about your draft that you think you can improve.

# 5. Revise

In this step of the writing process, you work on parts of your draft that need improvement. Use the peer review form that your classmate completed to help you. Also use your own ideas about how to improve each part of your informative text. This checklist includes some things to think about as you get ready to revise.

> ## Revision Checklist
>
> ✓ Does my introduction catch the reader's interest? Do I state the topic clearly?
>
> ✓ Are all of my details, facts, examples, and quotations important? Do they support my topic in a strong way?
>
> ✓ Is it clear where my facts, details, and examples come from? Have I cited my sources?
>
> ✓ Do I use transition words to connect my ideas and make the writing flow smoothly?
>
> ✓ Is my conclusion interesting? Have I restated my topic and summed up my ideas?

**STYLE AND TONE**
The style and tone of a piece of writing should fit the audience and subject. Underline words in this paragraph that fit an appropriate audience. How do you know the purpose of this piece is to give information rather than to be humorous?

_____

_____

## Writer's Craft: Style and Tone

When you write an informative text, the style and tone of your writing should be consistent as well as appropriate for your subject and audience. *Style* includes the words you use and the way you put words and sentences together. *Tone* is how you say something. You might use a serious tone for some pieces of writing and a funny tone for others. Now study the style and tone in this section of the mentor text.

When the Mayan center of Tikal was discovered in 1848, archaeologists—social scientists who study people and cultures from the past—found more than they had ever imagined. They realized that a mighty city lay buried beneath the layers of jungle growth. It had been deserted for hundreds of years.

# Try It!

**Revise Your Informative Text**

Reviewing the style and tone is an important part of revising an informative text. Practice using consistent style and tone with the following paragraph. Several sentences have problems with their style or tone. To make the style and tone consistent, rewrite sentences on the lines below the paragraph.

> (1) Machu Picchu is a really cool and really interesting ancient Inca site in Peru. (2) It was rediscovered by Hiram Bingham. (3) The site was rediscovered in 1911. (4) Today it is common and usual to find tourists exploring the remains of the beautiful and pretty city.

Sentence 1: _____

_____

Sentences 2 and 3: _____

_____

Sentence 4: _____

_____

## Writing Assignment

Now it is time to revise the draft of your informative text. Continue working on a computer or on a separate sheet of paper. Review the assignment and the checklist. Doing so will help you make sure that you have included everything you need to.

> The city of Pompeii in Italy is a site of ancient ruins. The city was partially buried by a volcanic eruption in 79 CE. Write at least five paragraphs describing Pompeii and its features. The text should include details from research texts and a conclusion.

# 6. Edit

After revising your informative text, you will edit it. When you edit, you read very carefully to be sure to find any mistakes in your writing. Here's a checklist of some things to look for as you edit.

**Editing Checklist**

✔ Did you indent each paragraph?

✔ Are all of your sentences complete? Does each have a subject and a verb?

✔ Did you begin each sentence with a capital letter?

✔ Does each sentence end with the correct punctuation?

✔ Have you used commas, colons, and semicolons correctly?

✔ Are all of your words spelled correctly?

You can use these editing marks to mark any errors you find.

| # Add space | ⌐ Indent | ^ Insert |
| 𝒫 Delete | ◯ Close up space | ≡ Capitalize |

This paragraph from the draft of the mentor text shows how to use editing marks.

⌐ Tikal also has several ball courts. Here, the Maya played a

game called pok-ta-pok. teams of men wore protective padding.
                                ≡

They played with a solid rubber ball. Winners received great
   #

riches, while members of the losing team might sometimes be

put two death.

# Language Focus: Spelling

**Spelling** is the correct arrangement of letters in a word. You can use some of the following general rules to spell words correctly.

| General Rule | Example |
|---|---|
| When adding a prefix, keep the spelling of the root word. | dis + loyal = disloyal |
| When adding a suffix that begins with a vowel to a word ending with a silent *e*, drop the *e*. | desire + -able = desirable |
| When adding a suffix that begins with a consonant to a word ending with a silent *e*, keep the *e*. | bare + ly = barely |
| When adding a suffix that begins with a vowel to a one-syllable word that ends in a single consonant, double the final consonant. | stop + ed = stopped |
| When making a noun that ends in *s*, *z*, *x*, *sh*, or *ch* plural, add -*es*. | dish = dishes |
| When making nouns ending in a vowel and *y* plural, add -*s*. | boy = boys |
| When making nouns ending in a consonant and *y* plural, drop the *y* and add -*ies*. | baby = babies |

Read the mentor text to find examples of correct spellings using the rules you just read.

(1) Tikal also has several ball courts. (2) Here, the Maya played a game called pok-ta-pok. (3) Teams of men wore protective padding as they played with a solid rubber ball. (4) Winners received great riches, while members of the losing team might sometimes face a death sentence!

**SPELLING** Read this section of the mentor text. Read rule 4 about doubling the final consonant. Underline the word in sentence 3 that follows this rule. Read rule 2 about dropping the *e*. Underline the word in sentence 4 that follows this rule. Circle the words that end with -*ed* and -*es*.

Edit **141**

# Try It!    Language and Editing Practice

For each sentence below, identify the spelling error and rewrite the word in the space provided.

1. Some of the churchs in the town want to help with flood relief.

   _____

2. Doctor, do you think it is unatural to be this hungry all the time?

   _____

3. The local grocery store sells organic turkeyes during the holidays.

   _____

4. The fifth-grade class collected quarters, dimes, nickels, and pennys for the charity drive.

   _____

Now use editing marks to correct the errors in this paragraph.

Ms. Daniels hired Kevin to help with several chores at her house? She had

heard from others in the neighborhood that he was very relyable. the first day

he showed up, she said, "Your first job is to find out why my trashcan keeps

dissappearing."

# Try It!   **Edit Your Informative Text**

Now edit your informative text. Use this checklist and the editing marks you have learned to correct any errors you find.

- ☐ Did you indent each paragraph?

- ☐ Are all of your sentences complete? Does each have a subject and a verb?

- ☐ Did you begin each sentence with a capital letter?

- ☐ Does each sentence end with the correct punctuation?

- ☐ Have you used commas, colons, and semicolons correctly?

- ☐ Are all of your words spelled correctly?

## Editing Tips

- Read your writing aloud. Add any missing words and correct any awkward-sounding sentences. Ask yourself, "Is that the best way to say this?"

- Reread your writing to make sure the style and tone are consistent.

- Read your writing over at a slow pace several times. Each time you read, focus on something different. For example, focus on punctuation in one reading and spelling in another reading.

# 7. Publish

On a computer or a separate sheet of paper, create a neat final draft of your informative text. Correct all errors that you identified while editing your draft. Be sure to give your informative text an interesting title.

The final step is to publish your informative text. Here are some different ways you might choose to share your work.

- Create a travel brochure featuring your informative text along with photos or illustrations of the city of Pompeii.

- Read your informative text aloud to your class, and compare and contrast it to other students' informative texts.

- Gather your informative text and the texts of other classmates into a booklet to share with a younger class.

- Read your informative text aloud to a family member. Ask the family member to list what he or she learned about Pompeii after hearing your piece.

**Technology Suggestions**
- Upload your informative text onto a class or school blog.
- Create a digital presentation of your informative text, and share it with the class.

# Reading Poetry

## Look at this river.

How do you think a poet might present ideas and feelings by referring to a river such as this one?

### ESSENTIAL QUESTION

*How do the themes in poetry help you gain a deeper understanding of nature and life in general?*

**Consider ▶** What are the two rivers that Emerson compares in the poem?

How does he feel about the two rivers?

# TWO RIVERS

*by Ralph Waldo Emerson*

**POETRY** Poetry is a literary form that often contains rhyming words. It also often arranges words in lines that have rhythm, or a repeated pattern of stressed and unstressed syllables. Sometimes poems are arranged in stanzas, which are groupings of lines. Why is it appropriate to refer to "Two Rivers" as poetry?

**POETIC CONTENT** Poetry often communicates ideas and feelings. What ideas and feelings are conveyed in lines 1–4?

**STANZAS AND THEME** A poem's theme is its central meaning. To identify the theme of a poem, you apply what you already know about nature, life, human nature, or society in general. What is this poem's theme? How does each stanza relate to and help you determine the poem's theme?

1  Thy summer voice, Musketaquit,[1]
Repeats the music of the rain;
But sweeter rivers pulsing flit
Through thee, as thou through Concord Plain.[2]

5  Thou in thy narrow banks art pent:
The stream I love unbounded goes
Through flood and sea and firmament;
Through light, through life, it forward flows.

I see the inundation sweet,
10  I hear the spending of the stream
Through years, through men, through Nature fleet,
Through love and thought, through power and dream.

[1]**Musketaquit** Native American name for the Concord River in Massachusetts

[2]**Concord Plain** the town of Concord, Massachusetts

Musketaquit, a goblin strong,
Of shard and flint makes jewels gay;
15   They lose their grief who hear his song,
And where he winds is the day of day.

So forth and brighter fares my stream,
Who drink it shall not thirst again;
No darkness stains its equal gleam,
20   And ages drop in it like rain.

**Ralph Waldo Emerson is a famous American author who lived from 1803 to 1882. He was a philosopher and the author of many poems, books, and essays.**

## Comprehension Check

Use the Venn diagram to compare and contrast the Musketaquit River and the river the speaker imagines in the poem. Think about the theme, and use details from the stanzas.

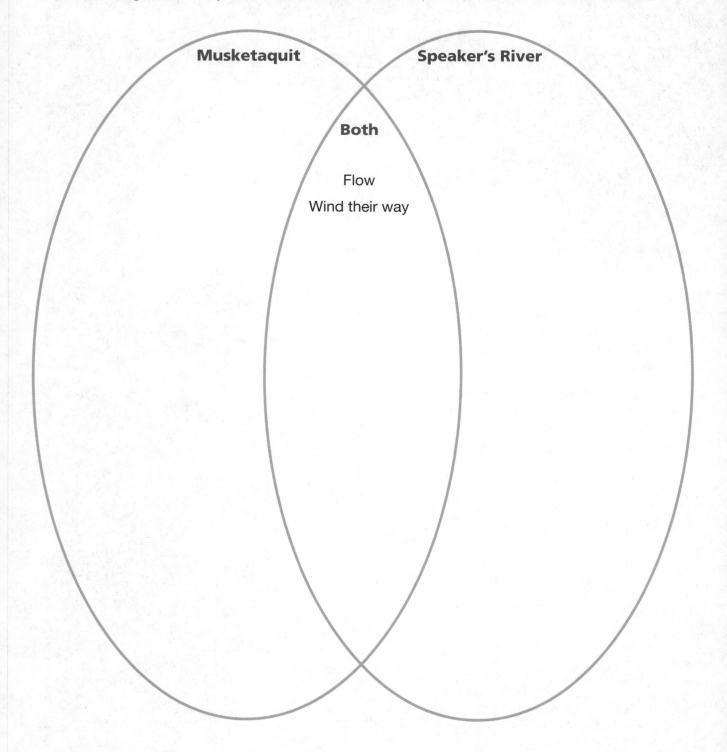

**Musketaquit**

**Speaker's River**

**Both**

Flow

Wind their way

## Vocabulary

Use the word map below to help you define and use one of the highlighted vocabulary words from the Share and Learn selection you are about to read or another word you choose.

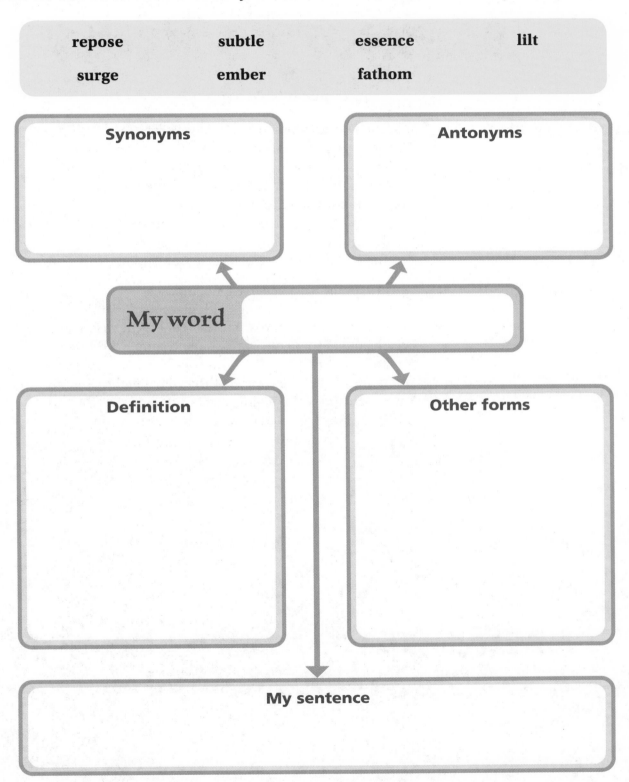

| repose | subtle | essence | lilt |
|---|---|---|---|
| surge | ember | fathom | |

**Synonyms**

**Antonyms**

**My word**

**Definition**

**Other forms**

**My sentence**

**Consider ▶**   What is memory's river?

How does the speaker think youth and adulthood are different?

# Memory's River

*by Ella Wheeler Wilcox*

**FIGURATIVE LANGUAGE**

What two things are being compared in line 11? What idea does this simile help convey?

_____

_____

_____

1    In Nature's bright blossoms not always reposes
     That strange subtle essence more rare than their bloom,
     Which lies in the hearts of carnations and roses,
     That unexplained something by men called perfume.

5    Though modest the flower, yet great is its power
     And pregnant with meaning each pistil and leaf,
     If only it hides there, if only abides there,
     The fragrance suggestive of love, joy, and grief.

     Not always the air that a master composes

10   Can stir human heart-strings with pleasure or pain.
     But strange, subtle chords, like the scent of the roses,
     Breathe out of some measures, though simple the strain.
     And lo! when you hear them, you love them and fear them,
     You tremble with anguish, you thrill with delight,

15   For back of them old dreams without number,
     And faces long vanished peer out into sight.

**FIGURATIVE LANGUAGE**

To what is the poet referring in lines 15–16?

_____

_____

_____

INFERENCES What can you infer about the speaker's feelings toward youth from the details in lines 17–24 and your own knowledge?

Those dear foolish days when the earth seemed all beauty,
Before you had knowledge enough to be sad;
When youth held no higher ideal of duty
20　Than just to lilt on through the world and be glad.
On harmony's river they seemed to float hither
With all the sweet fancies that hung round that time—
Life's burdens and troubles turn into air-bubbles
And break on the music's swift current of rhyme.

25　Fair Folly comes back with her spell while you listen
And points to the paths where she led you of old.
You gaze on past sunsets, you see dead stars glisten,
You bathe in life's glory, you swoon in death's cold.
All pains and all pleasures surge up through those measures,
30　Your heart is wrenched open with earthquakes of sound;
From ashes and embers rise Junes and Decembers,
Lost islands in fathoms of feeling refound.

POINT OF VIEW How does the poet develop the speaker's point of view about the power of music?

**INFERENCES** Where do the shipwrecks described in line 35 come from, and where do they go? What kinds of things from someone's past might be considered shipwrecks?

_____

_____

_____

**STANZAS AND THEME**
What do you think is the theme of this poem? Select two stanzas from the poem, and explain how the details in the stanzas support the theme.

_____

_____

_____

Some airs are like outlets of memory's oceans,
They rise in the past and flow into the heart;
35  And down them float shipwrecks of mighty emotions,
All sea-soaked and storm-tossed and drifting apart:
Their fair timbers battered, their lordly sails tattered,
Their skeleton crew of dead days on their decks;
Then a crash of chords blending, a crisis, an ending—
40  The music is over, and vanished the wrecks.

## Anchor Standard Discussion Questions

Discuss the following questions with your peer group. Then record your answers in the space provided.

1. How does the first stanza of "Memory's River" relate to the rest of the poem? Support your answer with details from the poem.

_____

_____

_____

_____

_____

_____

2. Do you think the speaker in "Memory's River" enjoys listening to the "strange, subtle chords" she describes? Support your answer with details from the poem.

_____

_____

_____

_____

_____

_____

## Comprehension Check

1.  What do you think "memory's river" refers to?

    _____

    _____

2.  The poet ends "Memory's River" with the phrase "and vanished the wrecks." What does the poet mean? Explain.

    _____

    _____

    _____

    _____

3.  Based on clues from the poem, do you think the speaker of the poem is a young person? Why or why not?

    _____

    _____

    _____

## Read On Your Own

Read another poem independently. Apply what you learned in this lesson and check your understanding.

# Writing Responses to Literature

## ESSENTIAL QUESTION

*How can analyzing a story's theme make a response to literature effective?*

**Did you like** the last story or book you read? Did it have an exciting plot, unforgettable characters, or a really interesting setting, maybe on another planet? Did you think that the theme or message of that story was especially meaningful? You can share your thoughts about a story by writing a response to literature. In this lesson, you will learn how to write an effective response to literature. You will each write your own response to the same two selections and then compare their themes.

# What's a Response to Literature?

You can write a response to any form of literature. Literature includes stories, plays, poems, books, and other forms of written work. One response might examine how the setting of a play affects its characters. Another response might compare two different forms of literature that approach the same theme or topic in similar or different ways.

A **response to literature** can be organized as a comparison and contrast essay. Read the ways to make your response to literature essay effective.

### Introduction
State your thesis—your opinion about the selections and the elements you are comparing and contrasting. Include the title and author (if available) of each one, and briefly summarize the selections. Introduce the points you will discuss in the next paragraphs.

### First Main Point and Supporting Details
State your first point or reason telling why your main idea is correct. Then support it with details from the texts.

### Second Main Point and Supporting Details
State your second point telling why your main idea is correct, and support it with details from the texts.

### Third Main Point and Supporting Details
State your third point telling why your main idea is correct, and support it with details from the texts.

### Conclusion
Repeat your thesis and summarize your main points. Leave the reader with some thoughts to consider.

## Analyze a Mentor Text: Reading

You will respond to two selections. One is "The Law of the Jungle," a poem from the novel *The Jungle Book* by Rudyard Kipling. The other selection is a story, "Looking into the Eyes of a Wolf." Read the two selections carefully before reviewing the mentor text writer's response to them on the following pages.

### "The Law of the Jungle"
### *from* The Jungle Book
### *by Rudyard Kipling*

*Now this is the Law of the Jungle—as old and as true as the sky;*
*And the Wolf that shall keep it may prosper, but the Wolf that shall break*
   *it must die.*
*As the creeper that girdles the tree-trunk the Law runneth forward*
   *and back—*
*For the strength of the Pack is the Wolf, and the strength of the Wolf is*
   *the Pack.*

Wash daily from nose-tip to tail-tip; drink deeply, but never too deep;
And remember the night is for hunting, and forget not the day is for sleep.
The Jackal may follow the Tiger, but, Cub, when thy whiskers are grown,
Remember the Wolf is a Hunter—go forth and get food of thine own.

Keep peace with the Lords of the Jungle—the Tiger, the Panther, the Bear.
And trouble not Hathi the Silent,[1] and mock not the Boar in his lair.
When Pack meets with Pack in the Jungle, and neither will go from
   the trail,
Lie down till the leaders have spoken—it may be fair words shall prevail.

When ye fight with a Wolf of the Pack, ye must fight him alone and afar,
Lest others take part in the quarrel, and the Pack be diminished
   by war.
The Lair of the Wolf is his refuge, and where he has made
   him his home,
Not even the Head Wolf may enter, not even the Council
   may come.

[1]**Hathi the Silent** a bull elephant

The Lair of the Wolf is his refuge, but where he has digged it too plain,
The Council shall send him a message, and so he shall change it again.
If ye kill before midnight, be silent, and wake not the woods with
    your bay,
Lest ye frighten the deer from the crop, and your brothers go empty away.

Ye may kill for yourselves, and your mates, and your cubs as they need,
    and ye can;
But kill not for pleasure of killing, and *seven times never kill Man!*
If ye plunder his Kill from a weaker, devour not all in thy pride;
Pack-Right is the right of the meanest; so leave him the head and
    the hide.

The Kill of the Pack is the meat of the Pack. Ye must eat where it lies;
And no one may carry away of that meat to his lair, or he dies.
The Kill of the Wolf is the meat of the Wolf. He may do what he will;
But, till he has given permission, the Pack may not eat of that Kill.

Cub-Right is the right of the Yearling. From all of his Pack he may claim
Full-gorge when the killer has eaten; and none may refuse him the same.
Lair-Right is the right of the Mother. From all of her year she may claim
One haunch of each kill for her litter, and none may deny her the same.

Cave-Right is the right of the Father—to hunt by himself for his own:
He is freed of all calls to the Pack; he is judged by the Council alone.
Because of his age and his cunning, because of his gripe and his paw,
In all that the Law leaveth open, the word of the Head Wolf is Law.

*Now these are the Laws of the Jungle,*
    *and many and mighty are they;*
*But the head and the hoof of the Law*
    *and the haunch and the hump is—Obey!*

# Looking into the Eyes of a Wolf

Wei Ling was brimming with excitement. She had recently moved to Raleigh-Durham, North Carolina, because her mother had taken a job with the U.S. Fish and Wildlife Service (FWS). The previous night her best friend, Elena, had arrived for a visit. Wei Ling couldn't wait to show Elena the Alligator National Wildlife Refuge, where her mother worked on the red wolf restoration project.

While Wei Ling's mother drove them to the refuge, she explained that in 1987 the Alligator River Refuge became the first place anyone had ever attempted to reintroduce a large carnivore to its native range. Once, red wolves had lived throughout the southeastern United States. However, they were overhunted and overtrapped. People developed the land, so that by 1970, the red wolf was the world's most endangered carnivore. There were fewer than one hundred red wolves left alive, all of them in Texas and Louisiana.

"The red wolves were interbreeding with coyotes," Wei Ling's mother said. "If this continued, they would disappear as a species forever."

Wei Ling's mother explained how the FWS worked to prevent the extinction of the wolves. In 1975, the FWS got permission to capture all the remaining wild wolves and test them to see whether they were true red wolves or a combination of red wolf and coyote. Then they bred the pure wolves.

"How many wolves are there where we're going?" Wei Ling asked.

"There may be as many as one hundred," her mother answered. "The Alligator River Refuge, which covers 152,000 acres, is the heart of the project, but the wolf restoration area includes a million acres!" Then Wei Ling's mother explained that the FWS chose to reintroduce the wolves in areas far from people.

"I hope we get to see some of the wolves," Elena said.

"Don't be disappointed if you don't," Wei Ling's mother warned as they finally arrived at the refuge. "The wolves try to avoid people. I'll see you back here in an hour," Wei Ling's mother said. "Remember, don't wander off the trails!"

Wei Ling rolled her eyes and laughed. She grabbed Elena's arm and headed toward the woods. The girls walked for a long time. Suddenly, Wei Ling stopped. "Don't move," she whispered.

Just fifty or sixty feet ahead of them, two red wolves stood over the carcass of a deer. There was blood on the wolves' muzzles—it was a fresh kill. The wolves had long, slim legs and cinnamon-colored fur. With their large ears flicked forward, their heads held low, and their tails standing up, they glared at the girls. One growled softly, showing its long canine teeth.

Wei Ling thought of everything her mother had told her about what to do if she ever met wolves. *Never approach them,* her mother had said. *Move slowly away. Don't turn and run.* It was hard not to run. She was terrified!

"Back up very slowly," Wei Ling whispered. "Don't run."

"I want to get out of here," Elena whispered back.

"Let's just keep backing up," Wei Ling said softly. She reached out to touch Elena's arm. They walked backward, very slowly, until the wolves were out of sight. Then they turned and ran.

After a few minutes, they stopped to catch their breath. "I've never been so scared in my life!" said Elena.

Wei Ling felt ready to burst with excitement. Beaming, she said, "I think that this was the luckiest day of my life!"

## Analyze a Mentor Text: Response

This is an example of an effective response to the two selections by a sixth grader. Read it and then complete the activities in the boxes as a class.

### Wolves in Literature

Wolves have been depicted in various ways in literature. Two pieces of literature that have differing depictions of wolves are "The Law of the Jungle" by Rudyard Kipling and "Looking into the Eyes of a Wolf." In "The Law of the Jungle," Rudyard Kipling writes about the rules that wolves must follow because they are part of a pack. In "Looking into the Eyes of a Wolf," the author writes about two girls who go walking in a refuge for wolves and see two of them eating a deer. The poem depicts the wolves as almost human, having little contact with people, and behaving in orderly ways. The story, on the other hand, depicts the wolves as real animals who have been harmed and helped by people and can also be dangerous to humans.

Kipling's poem "The Law of the Jungle" mentions people only once, when the speaker says that "the law of the jungle" is never to kill people. "Looking into the Eyes of a Wolf," however, focuses on the effects of human activities on wolves' survival. The story explains how people have overhunted and overtrapped wolves. Humans have also taken over much of the land where red wolves used to live, causing them to become endangered. This story also tells how the U.S. Fish and Wildlife Service (FWS) is now trying to save the wolves from extinction.

In the poem, Kipling gives the wolves positive human traits, such as fighting fairly, respecting elders, and sharing meat with the pack. In the story, however, the wolves are shown eating their kill and growling to keep the girls away from it. The author depicts them as ordinary animals and does not give them human traits.

**INTRODUCTION** The introduction includes a thesis statement of the most important idea. In writing a response to literature, the thesis is the writer's opinion about an aspect of literature. The writer also names and briefly summarizes both selections. Draw a line under the sentence that compares the way the two selections portray wolves.

**SUPPORTING DETAILS** Paragraph 2 describes the first way that the two selections are different. Underline the details that were taken from the story.

**SUPPORTING DETAILS**
Why does the mentor text writer include the sentence about Wei Ling's fear?

**CONCLUSION** The conclusion summarizes the mentor text writer's main points discussed in the essay. How is the thesis restated?

The poem focuses on the orderly way that a wolf pack governs itself. It gives examples of the rules that wolves obey. In contrast, the story depicts wolves as wild and unpredictable. Although Wei Ling remembers that wolves attack only when people run, she is still terrified as she backs away. She is also excited!

In conclusion, while both authors focus on wolves, they portray them very differently in the selections. Kipling's poem treats the wolves as characters that follow rules and seem almost human, though they have little or no contact with humans. The story describes wolves as real, exciting, and sometimes dangerous animals that have been both harmed and helped by humans. The writers of both selections clearly admire these amazing animals.

**Think About It ▶** In your opinion, which reason in the response to literature is the most convincing? What other supporting details could the writer have included?

# Vocabulary Study: Denotation and Connotation

**Denotation** is the literal meaning or dictionary definition of a word. **Connotation** is the feeling, or emotion, that certain words convey or produce. This feeling could be positive or negative. In the chart below, each pair of words in parentheses has a similar denotation. One of the words in each pair has a positive or negative connotation, and the other is neutral. Write each word in the appropriate column. For unfamiliar words, use a dictionary.

| Examples | Positive | Negative | Neutral |
|---|---|---|---|
| Ellie was (content/excited) on the last day of school. | excited | | content |
| The meal portions in the restaurant are (small/microscopic). | | | |
| Expect (high/sweltering) temperatures in July. | | | |
| The (breeze/wind) knocked over the garbage cans. | | | |
| Devon (hurt/tweaked) his ankle during the dash. | | | |

Read these sentences. Decide whether the underlined word in each sentence has a positive or a negative connotation. Write the word in the appropriate column.

| Mentor Text Sentence | Positive | Negative |
|---|---|---|
| Humans have also taken over much of the land where red wolves used to live, causing them to become <u>endangered</u>. | | |
| In the story, however, the wolves are shown eating their kill and <u>growling</u> to keep the girls away from it. | | |
| The poem focuses on the <u>orderly</u> way that a wolf pack governs itself. | | |

# Writing Process

Now that you have read and analyzed a response to literature, you are going to create your own response. You will follow these steps of the writing process.

**1. Get Ready: Brainstorm** Think about the themes of both selections, and brainstorm possible statements that compare them. Choose the best comparison, in your opinion. Brainstorm reasons why that comparison is correct, and choose the three strongest reasons. Gather supporting evidence for your reasons.

**2. Organize** Use a graphic organizer to organize the main points and supporting details.

**3. Draft** Create the first draft of your response to literature.

**4. Peer Review** Work with a partner to evaluate and improve your draft.

**5. Revise** Use suggestions from your peer review to revise your response.

**6. Edit** Check your work carefully for errors in spelling, punctuation, and grammar.

**7. Publish** Create a final version of your response to literature.

## Writing Assignment

In this lesson, you will write your own response to literature. As you create the piece, remember the elements of the mentor text that were most effective. Read the following assignment.

> Compare and contrast the themes of the poem "The Law of the Jungle" and the story "Looking into the Eyes of a Wolf." What is the theme of each selection, and how are these themes similar and different? Support your response with details from the selections.

# 1. Get Ready: Brainstorm

When you brainstorm, you think of as many ideas as you can and record them. Don't edit your ideas—just let them flow.

For this response to literature, the mentor text writer first reread the selections and paid attention to how wolves are depicted. Then the writer used the graphic organizer below to jot down ideas.

| Selection | How Wolves Are Depicted |
|---|---|
| "The Law of the Jungle" | proud, part of a family, follow strict laws, fight fairly, kill only when they need to eat, respect older wolves |
| "Looking into the Eyes of a Wolf" | threatened by human actions, nearly extinct, now protected in a refuge, exciting to see, dangerous |

Then the mentor text writer used those notes to compare and contrast how wolves were portrayed in both selections. The writer looked for similarities and differences. These became the main idea for this writer's response to the literature.

## Try It!    Use a Graphic Organizer for Brainstorming

To begin this assignment, you need to identify the theme of each selection. Reread each work. What lesson or main idea does the author want readers to remember? Use the graphic organizer below for your notes.

| Selection | Possible Themes |
|---|---|
| "The Law of the Jungle" | |
| "Looking into the Eyes of a Wolf" | |

# Brainstorm Ideas for Your Response

Next, you need to identify three main ways that the themes of the selections are similar or different, which will form your thesis. The mentor text writer used the idea web below to brainstorm points to support the thesis for the mentor response.

**THESIS** Make your main point clear.

**MAIN POINTS** Choose three strong points that support your thesis. You may add to or revise your reasons as you draft your response.

**SUPPORTING DETAILS** Provide details to support your points. Later, you can choose the best details to use in your response.

**Thesis:**
The selections depict wolves differently.

**Main Point 1**
Difference: "Eyes" tells how humans affect wolves.

**Main Point 2**
Difference: "Law" makes wolves seem human.

**Main Point 3**
Difference: "Law" shows wolves as orderly and predictable.

**Supporting Details**

"Law" shows how wolves respect humans.

"Eyes" tells how humans threaten wolves and how FWS works to save them.

**Supporting Details**

"Law" tells about wolves fighting fair and respecting elders.

"Eyes" depicts wolves as ordinary animals that kill prey and protect their food.

**Supporting Details**

"Law" describes wolves following rules.

"Eyes" describes Wei Ling's reactions to seeing the wolves.

# Try It!

**Use a Graphic Organizer for Brainstorming**

Now use the idea web below to brainstorm main points and supporting details for your comparison of the themes in your response to literature.

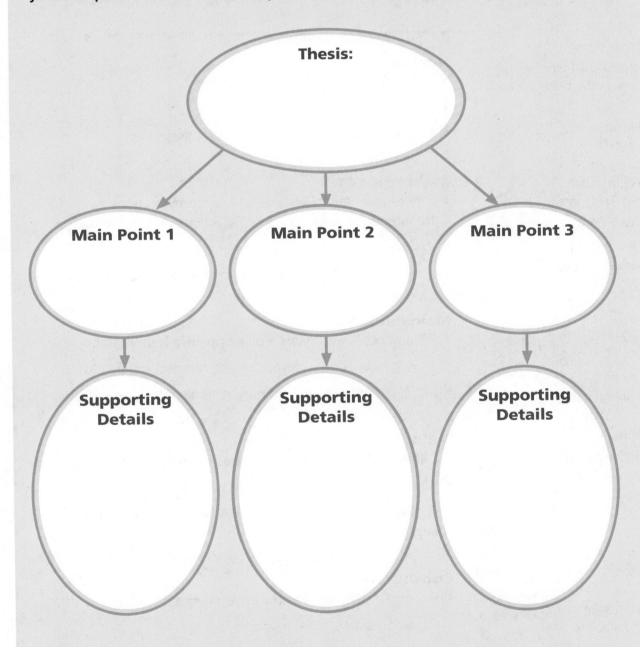

# 2. Organize

You are almost ready to begin a draft of your response. A more detailed graphic organizer can help you organize your ideas into the best order or sequence. You can then refer to this graphic organizer as you write your draft. The writer of the mentor text completed this graphic organizer:

## INTRODUCTION
Summaries should be one or two sentences. Be sure to

- include only information necessary for readers to under-stand the response
- state your thesis
- introduce reasons that support thesis

## SUPPORTING PARAGRAPHS
Be sure to

- state your main points and show how each supports the thesis
- support each point with details from the selections

## CONCLUSION
Be sure to

- restate your thesis and summarize your main points
- give something for reader to consider

### Introduction
- Titles and authors; brief summaries
- Wolves portrayed differently
- List of three main points to be discussed

### Main Point #1
- Difference: Only "Eyes" tells how human actions have threatened wolves and how FWS is trying to save them.
- Include details about the human actions.
- "Law" mentions humans once; no focus on humans/wolves.

### Main Point #2
- Difference: "Law" gives wolves positive human traits.
- Kipling tells about wolves fighting fair, respecting elders.
- In "Eyes," wolves are ordinary animals. They eat a deer.

### Main Point #3
- Difference: Only "Law" describes the wolves' orderly lives.
- Kipling describes the rules that wolves live by.
- In "Eyes," Wei Ling is afraid of wolves because of their unpredictability.

### Conclusion
- Restate thesis: Wolves portrayed differently
- Summarize the three main points.

# Try It!    **Organize Your Response to Literature**

Now use the graphic organizer below to organize the points and details you want to include in each paragraph of your draft.

**Introduction**

**Main Point 1 and Supporting Details**

**Main Point 2 and Supporting Details**

**Main Point 3 and Supporting Details**

**Conclusion**

# 3. Draft

Now it is time to begin the first draft of your response to literature. Remember, your goal is to get your ideas down—either on paper or on a computer—in an organized way. You can pay attention to spelling, punctuation, grammar, and other issues later, when you revise your writing.

## Writer's Craft: Using Linking Words

Linking words, or transitions, can show the relationship between ideas. They can make writing flow more smoothly. Here are some examples:

| | |
|---|---|
| Linking words that show *addition* | also, too, in addition, and, besides |
| Linking words that show *contrast* | however, on the other hand, still, but |
| Linking words that show *a reason or cause* | because, therefore, as a result, since |
| Linking words that show *time* | then, next, first, second, finally, when |
| Linking words that *give examples* | for example, for instance, such as |

Notice how the writer of the mentor text uses linking words.

**TRANSITIONS**
Which transitions does the mentor text writer use to combine ideas and show the relationship among them?

In the poem, Kipling gives the wolves positive human traits, such as fighting fairly, respecting elders, and sharing meat with the pack. In the story, however, the wolves are shown eating their kill and growling to keep the girls away from it. The author depicts them as ordinary animals and does not give them human traits.

# Try It!　Write Your First Draft

On a computer or on a separate sheet of paper, create the draft of your response to literature. Remember to use linking words to connect your ideas. This drafting checklist can help as you write.

✓ In your introduction, include the titles and brief summaries of the selections. Clearly state your thesis, comparing and contrasting the themes. List the three main points that you will explain and that support your thesis.

✓ In each of the next three paragraphs, support your thesis, comparing and contrasting the themes. Start each paragraph by stating your main point. Then provide details from the selections to support your main point.

✓ In your conclusion, stress how your three main points prove that your comparison of the themes is correct.

✓ Use linking words to show how the ideas in your sentences are related.

## Tips for Writing Your First Draft

- Remember that you do not have to start writing with your introduction. You can start with your main points and write your introduction last.
- Think about the best order for your three main points. Usually, writers place the strongest point first.
- Write down key phrases and ideas before you begin your draft. This is a good way to get started.

# 4. Peer Review

After you write your draft, you and a partner will review each other's responses. Here is a draft of the mentor text. Read it with your partner and answer the questions in the boxes. On the next page, you will find out how the mentor text writer's partner evaluated this draft.

**INTRODUCTION**
These summaries need a few more details to make them clear. Also, the thesis does not clearly state how wolves are portrayed in the selections. How should the writer end this paragraph?

**MAIN POINT**
The writer explains how "Looking into the Eyes of a Wolf" describes the effects of human actions on wolves. What else should the writer do to make this first point effective?

**CONCLUSION** The writer repeats some of the main points in the conclusion. What else could the writer add to make the conclusion stronger?

In "The Law of the Jungle," Rudyard Kipling writes about the rules that wolves must follow. In "Looking into the Eyes of a Wolf," the author writes about two girls who find wolves eating a deer. The selections are different in three ways.

Only the author of "Looking into the Eyes of a Wolf" describes how humans have threatened wolves. This story tells how the U.S. Fish and Wildlife Service is trying to save the wolves from extinction. The author explains that people have overhunted and overtrapped wolves. Humans have also taken over much of the land where wolves lived, causing them to become endangered.

Kipling gives wolves human traits. He says they fight fairly and respect elders. They also have rules about sharing meat with the pack. The wolves in the other selection are ordinary animals.

The poem focuses on how wolves govern themselves, while the story depicts wolves as wild animals that can be dangerous. In the story, Wei Ling remembers that wolves attack only when people run. She is still terrified as she backs away. She is also excited by the encounter.

These two selections show wolves as characters in a poem and as real animals in a story. Only one selection tells how humans have threatened wolves. Only Kipling makes wolves seem almost human.

# Sample Peer Review Form

This peer review form shows how a partner evaluated the draft of the mentor text shown on the previous page.

| | |
|---|---|
| **The introduction states the selection titles.** | You did a good job of naming the selections. |
| **The writer summarizes the selections with enough details to help readers understand the response and states the thesis.** | You could improve your response by adding details to the summaries and the thesis. It's not clear that you are comparing how wolves are portrayed in the selections. |

| | |
|---|---|
| **The next three paragraphs provide a supporting main point for the thesis.** | You did a good job of choosing three points that support your main idea. |
| **The writer uses evidence from the text in each main point.** | You could improve your response by mentioning both selections in each paragraph, because you are comparing them. |

| | |
|---|---|
| **The writer uses transitions to show the relationships among ideas.** | You did a good job of using "while" in several places to contrast the treatment in the poem with the treatment in the story. |
| | You could improve your response by using more transition words throughout your response. For example, you could combine some short sentences in the fourth paragraph. |

| | |
|---|---|
| **The conclusion stresses how the three points support the thesis.** | You did a good job of repeating two of your main points. |
| | You could improve your response by restating your thesis and adding the third main point. |

# Try It!    **Peer Review with a Partner**

Now you will work with a partner to review each other's response drafts. Use the peer review form below. If you need help, look back at the peer review form on the previous page.

| | |
|---|---|
| **The introduction states the selection titles.**<br><br>**The writer summarizes the selections with enough details to help readers understand the response and states the thesis.** | You did a good job of<br><br>You could improve your response by |
| **The next three paragraphs provide a supporting main point for the thesis.**<br><br>**The writer uses evidence from the text in each main point.** | You did a good job of<br><br>You could improve your response by |
| **The writer uses transitions to show the relationships among ideas.** | You did a good job of<br><br>You could improve your response by |
| **The conclusion stresses how the three points support the thesis.** | You did a good job of<br><br>You could improve your response by |

# Try It!

**Record Key Peer Review Comments**

Now it is time for you and your partner to share your comments with each other. Listen to your partner's feedback, and write his or her key comments in the left column. Then write some ideas for improving your draft in the right column.

| | |
|---|---|
| My reviewer says that my introduction | I will |
| My reviewer says that my first main point | I will |
| My reviewer says that my second main point | I will |
| My reviewer says that my third main point | I will |
| My reviewer says that my use of linking words is | I will |
| My reviewer says that my conclusion | I will |

Use the space below to write other things that you can do to improve your draft.

# 5. Revise

In this step of the writing process, you find ways to make your response stronger and clearer. The peer review form that your partner completed can help. Be sure to use your own ideas about how to improve your writing. This checklist includes things to think about as you revise.

---

**Revision Checklist**

✓ Does my introduction clearly state my thesis? Do I include the titles and authors (if available) of the literature? Do I briefly summarize the selections? Do I introduce the three main points I will use to support my thesis?

✓ Does my first paragraph discuss a strong point or reason for my thesis? Do I use evidence from the text to support this point?

✓ Do my next two paragraphs discuss two more strong points for my thesis? Do I include evidence to support each point?

✓ Do I conclude by restating my thesis? Do I stress how my main points support my thesis?

✓ Do I use linking words to show the relationships among my ideas?

---

**VARYING SENTENCE STRUCTURE**

Varying length and types of sentences makes writing more interesting. Underline the longest sentence. Box the sentence that is not a statement. Circle the sentence that begins with a linking word.

## Writer's Craft: Varying Sentence Structure

Writing is more interesting when the sentences are not all the same. Some can start with an introductory word, phrase, or clause, or a sentence can be a question or an exclamation. Some sentences can be short, and some long.

Look at the mentor text for examples of varied sentence structure.

The poem focuses on the orderly way that a wolf pack governs itself. It gives examples of the rules that wolves obey. In contrast, the story depicts wolves as wild and unpredictable. Although Wei Ling remembers that wolves attack only when people run, she is terrified as she backs away. She is also excited!

# Try It!

**Revise Your Response to Literature**

Varying your sentence structure will make your writing more interesting—for you as well as your readers. Revise the paragraph that follows to vary the sentence structure.

> They lifted the lid of the box. They could not believe their eyes. Inside was something valuable and amazing. At first, they showed no reaction. They did not want anyone else in the room to know how surprised and delighted they were. It was their surprise to share.

_____

_____

_____

_____

_____

## Writing Assignment

Continue working on a computer or on a separate sheet of paper. Review the assignment, repeated below, and the checklist. Doing so will help you make sure that you have included everything you need to.

> Compare and contrast the themes of the poem "The Law of the Jungle" and the story "Looking into the Eyes of a Wolf." What is the theme of each selection, and how are these themes similar and different? Support your response with details from the selections.

# 6. Edit

After revising your response to literature, you will edit it. You will read carefully to find any mistakes. Here's a checklist of things to look for as you edit.

---

**Editing Checklist**

✔ Did you indent each paragraph?

✔ Are all of your sentences complete, with a subject and a verb? Did you divide any run-on sentences?

✔ Does each sentence end with the correct punctuation?

✔ Have you used commas, colons, and semicolons correctly?

✔ Are all of the words spelled correctly?

---

You can use these editing marks to mark any errors you find.

| | |
|---|---|
| ⊙ Insert period | ⟳ Close up space |
| ∩ Reverse order | # Add space |
| ⌃ Insert comma | ⟋ Delete |

This paragraph from the draft of the mentor text shows how to use editing marks.

> Only the author of "Looking into the Eyes of a Wolf"
>
> describes how humans have thraetened wolves. This story tells
>
> how the U.S. Fish and Wild life Service is is trying to save the
>
> wolves from extinction. The author explains that poeple have
>
> overhunted and overtrapped wolves. Humans have also
>
> takenover much of the land where wolves lived causing them
>
> to become endangered

## Language Focus: Vague Pronouns

A **pronoun** takes the place of a noun. However, writers need to be clear, not vague, about what noun a pronoun replaces. Read this sentence.

> Jeff called to tell Jamal that he was on the team.

Who is on the team, Jeff or Jamal? The pronoun *he* could refer to either Jeff or Jamal. Here are two revisions of this sentence, both of which make it clearer.

> Jeff found out that Jamal was on the team and called to tell him. (**Jamal** *is on the team.*)
>
> Jeff found out that he was on the team and called to tell Jamal. (**Jeff** *is on the team.*)

Here's another pronoun that is vague.

> My birthday party was lots of fun, and I got a new phone. I texted my cousin about it.

Did the writer text about the birthday party or the new phone? To which noun does the pronoun *it* refer? This sentence does not make the answer clear.

When you write, make sure each pronoun refers to a specific noun.

> In the poem, Kipling gives the wolves positive human traits, such as fighting fairly, respecting elders, and sharing meat with the pack. In the story, however, the wolves are shown eating their kill and growling to keep the girls away from it. The author depicts them as ordinary animals and does not give them human traits.

**PRONOUNS** Read this section of the mentor text. Each pronoun must refer to a specific noun. Circle each pronoun in the paragraph, and underline the word it refers to.

# Try It!     Language and Editing Practice

Read each sentence. If the underlined pronoun refers to a specific noun, mark the sentence C for *clear*. If the underlined pronoun is vague, rewrite the sentence.

1. A few people tried to get on the train, but <u>they</u> could not fit.

_____

_____

2. Louisa asked Ms. Teele if <u>she</u> had the latest schedule.

_____

_____

3. While Kevin was practicing, his brother studied <u>his</u> notes.

_____

_____

**Now use editing marks to correct the errors in this paragraph.**

He left his apartment building swiftly in order to make it to the trainstation on

time. The journey was going to be a long one and he did not want to be late.

Seven years ago when he went on the same trip he was a lot younger and not

as eagre. This time he knew exactly what to expect and he could not wait.

The excitement was over whelming.

# Try It!    **Edit Your Response to Literature**

Now edit your response to literature. Use this checklist and the editing marks you have learned to correct any errors you find.

☐ Did you indent each paragraph?

☐ Are all of your sentences complete, with a subject and a verb? Did you divide any run-on sentences?

☐ Did you use transition words to show the relationships between your ideas?

☐ Did you vary your sentence structure?

☐ Do your pronouns clearly refer to specific nouns?

☐ Does each sentence end with the correct punctuation?

☐ Are all of the words spelled correctly?

## Editing Tips

- Read your response slowly aloud. If a few sentences sound short and choppy, see if you can combine some of your ideas.

- Remember that you will probably not find many errors with one quick read. Take your time and read through your response slowly two or three times.

- If possible, put your response aside for a few hours or overnight. When you read it again, your eyes—and brain—will be fresh. Then you will be more likely to find errors.

# 7. Publish

Using a computer or a separate sheet of paper, create a neat final draft of your response to literature. Correct all errors that you identified while editing. Be sure to give your response an interesting title.

The final step is to publish and share your work, perhaps using one of these ideas:

- In a small group, read your responses aloud. Compare your responses. How are they similar and different? Discuss whether you would like to read other selections by the same authors. Why or why not?

- Display the class responses on a bulletin board.

- Create a poster that includes your own drawing or other artwork for each selection. Try to express your ideas about the selections in the drawings. Display the drawings side by side.

## Technology Suggestions

- **Upload your response to literature onto a class or school blog.**
- **Use a computer to add graphics, a border, colored text, interesting fonts, or clip art to your own response to literature or to the class display on the bulletin board.**

# Reading Persuasive Nonfiction

**Look at this** girl playing soccer. How do you think players and their families might feel if there were no soccer teams for some of the players?

## ESSENTIAL QUESTION

*How can persuasive nonfiction use reasoned judgments and facts to influence readers?*

**Consider ▶** Should boys and girls have the opportunity to play together on the same team?

Should these mixed-gender teams be required to have minimum numbers of boys and girls?

# Co-ed CONFLICT

**PERSUASIVE NONFICTION**
Persuasive nonfiction is writing that states an argument in support of a writer's point of view about an issue or topic. What is the topic for this persuasive nonfiction selection?

1    Sports play is an important part of teaching and learning about fitness and fairness. Many sports teams play for the schools within our district. Most of the members of these teams devote an extraordinary amount of time, effort, and dedication to their sports and schools. Should these players be penalized when circumstances beyond their control take away one of their players during each game?

A debate is raging about the fairness of the Ridgeview School District's rules and regulations for its indoor soccer league. Rules specify that each team must have at least two players of each gender. The rules also require that at least one male player and one female player be active on the field at all times during the game. Any team that fails to meet this requirement must forfeit one player during the game.

A problem arises, however, due to the fact that at some schools, no girls have chosen to join the soccer team. This means that the team must lose a player in every game. The coaches, parents, and students at these schools feel strongly that this is unfair. This rule means that the opposing team always has an advantage. In effect, it penalizes a team even though its players have not broken any rules.

Many community members have written letters to state their points of view about the policy. Two of the letters appear here.

**Letter 1**

Dear Editor:

5    The Ridgeview School District's insistence on co-ed teams in the indoor soccer league has clearly resulted in a policy that is unrealistic and unfair. According to this policy, each team must be balanced. Although our team, the Lee School Leopards, has tried its utmost to encourage girls to join, we have been unsuccessful. While there are girls on many sports teams at our school, their preference must be to play sports other than soccer, as none of them have joined our school's soccer team. Our team is always penalized.

**POINT OF VIEW** Point of view is the writer's perspective about a topic or issue. A writer can be for or against a topic or issue. You can often tell by the words a writer uses what his or her point of view is. What is Patrick's point of view about co-ed soccer teams? Is he for them or against them? What words tell you?

**ARGUMENT** An argument is the main idea that expresses the author's point of view in persuasive nonfiction. What argument does Patrick make that supports his point of view?

**CLAIMS** A claim is a statement a writer makes to support an argument. Some claims may be supported by reasons and evidence. What claims has Patrick stated that support his argument?

**EVALUATE EVIDENCE**  To build a strong persuasive argument, an author must provide relevant and reliable evidence that supports his or her claims. The evidence may include facts, examples, and illustrations. Does the evidence in each underlined sentence provide strong support for Patrick's claims?

**AUTHOR'S PURPOSE**  Every author writes for one or more purposes. Authors usually write to explain, express, inform, or persuade. What is Patrick's main purpose, and how does it relate to his point of view?

No sports teams could keep a positive outlook with this negative policy in place. This policy makes it harder for us to compete against some other teams in our district. <u>Since we have no girls on our team, we must forfeit a player at each game.</u> The policy also makes the game less fun. For example, our outnumbered players have to work exceedingly hard to protect their goal. <u>In one game, so many players were around our goal that it came crashing down on them; someone could have been injured.</u> The district should change to an all-boys and an all-girls league now. That is the only way to be impartial to all teams.

Sincerely,

Patrick Soliz

**Letter 2**

Dear Editor:

Calls for an all-boys and all-girls indoor soccer league in the Ridgeview School District are unwise. They run against the district's mission of providing equal opportunities for all students. My daughter has played soccer on the El Portal School team for three years, which has been an exceedingly valuable experience. The team spirit she shares with her teammates—the boys and the girls—is special. She has learned how to work as part of a team. In one game, she gave up the possibility of a goal for herself because she thought the team had a better chance at the championship if she let someone else on her team go for the goal. Some people argue that we should change to all-boys and all-girls leagues to avoid unfairly penalizing teams that have too few girls. However, if we do this, we will create a greater injustice. My daughter and the other female players would be unable to play at all, since there are just not enough interested girls.

Changing the league now would be completely unfair. It would eradicate any opportunity my daughter could ever have to understand fairness in sports. Sports teams without girls need to take new and innovative measures to encourage girls to join. When the teams succeed in such an endeavor, then players will succeed in learning about teamwork and fairness to players of both genders. The league's rules were formed for a reason. They are strong and work well. Without a doubt, they should be upheld.

Sincerely,

Lin Tran

**ELABORATE KEY IDEAS**
Authors make arguments for their point of view by providing reasons and facts. They also elaborate on those reasons by providing examples and illustrations. What example does Lin provide in this letter to show how the current policy has made her daughter a strong team player?

**PERSUASIVE TECHNIQUE**
Authors strengthen their arguments by including opposing facts or opinions and refuting, or arguing against, them. In which sentence does Lin present an opposing argument and refute it?

## Comprehension Check

Complete the chart below, using information from the two letters. List the facts and evidence that are in favor of the current policy in the "Pro" column. List the facts and evidence that are against the current policy in the "Con" column. Then answer the question that follows.

| Pro | Con |
|---|---|
| The current policy provides an equal opportunity for all students. | The current policy makes it harder for teams with no girls to be competitive. |
| | |
| | |

Which letter presents a stronger argument for its author's point of view? Explain.

_____

_____

_____

# Vocabulary

Use the word map below to help you define and use one of the highlighted vocabulary words from the Share and Learn selection you are about to read or another word you choose.

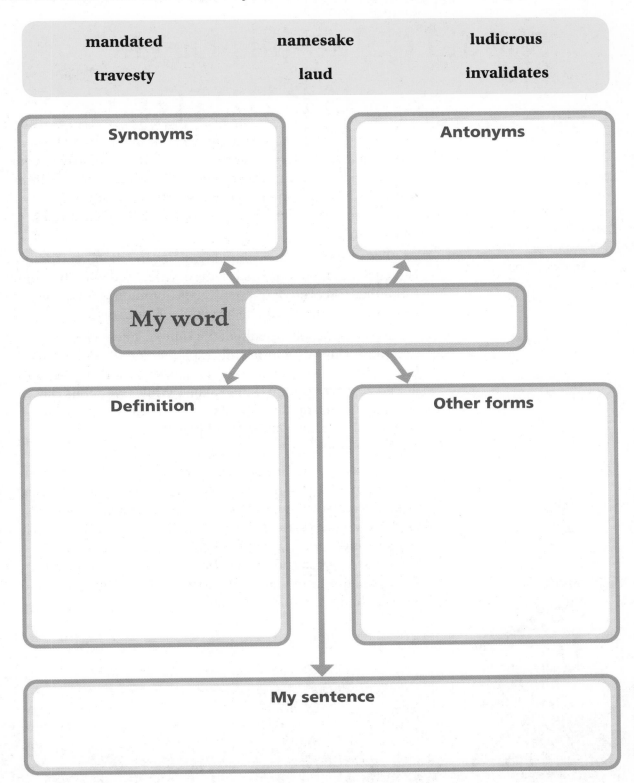

mandated     namesake     ludicrous

travesty     laud     invalidates

**Synonyms**

**Antonyms**

**My word**

**Definition**

**Other forms**

**My sentence**

**Consider ▶** Who really discovered America?

What was the role of Christopher Columbus in history?

# Should Columbus Day be
# Renamed?

1    "In fourteen hundred ninety-two, Columbus sailed the ocean blue. . . ." This familiar rhyme reminds us of the man who "discovered" America: Christopher Columbus. He and his three ships, the *Niña*, the *Pinta*, and the *Santa Maria*, are as much a part of America's history and identity as the stars and stripes. Or are they?

Because of the curriculum mandated in schools across the United States for decades, students have learned that Christopher Columbus discovered America. But is Columbus's "discovery" worthy of a celebration? Did he genuinely earn his fame?

Many students throughout the United States celebrate Columbus Day by honoring this explorer. And the Columbus Day holiday provides a day off—a break from work and school duties—for many in the United States. While Columbus Day is not celebrated on the same day in all states, it is generally celebrated at some point in October in recognition of the holiday's namesake.

Increasingly, Columbus and his place in American history have come under the microscope. By the time Columbus sailed to America, Native Americans had already inhabited the land for thousands of years, so many say that the idea of Columbus "discovering" America is ludicrous. Many state that Columbus arrived in America and treated the Native Americans he met as slaves, stealing from them and harming them, all in an effort to advance his own career and goals.

**CONNOTATION** Look at the word *recognition* in paragraph 3. What does the word imply, and how does it make you feel about the topic?

_____

_____

_____

5    Many hold the belief that celebrating Columbus for having committed crimes against America's native people is a travesty. They feel strongly that celebrating Columbus Day shows a lack of respect for Native Americans and even for previous explorers. The Norsemen Leif Ericson and Bjarni Herjólfsson may have sighted America centuries before Columbus sailed west.

Across the nation, Columbus Day festivities have been on the wane. In some communities, this is not a comment on Columbus himself but rather on the insignificance of the holiday. Some even say the holiday has become unimportant because it celebrates the wrong person.

What are the sides of the debate? Is Columbus Day worth celebrating or not?

*Christopher Columbus*

**The topic:** The name of Columbus Day should be changed.

**Con:**

8    Columbus Day should remain just as it has been since it became a national holiday in 1937. The idea that the holiday's name should be changed is senseless. We should continue to honor Christopher Columbus, his exploration, and the discoveries he made—even if he made them in a dishonorable way. We believe that a change would undermine the foundation of our nation.

It is true that Columbus's exploration led to conquistadors entering America and taking the lives of millions of Native Americans. We also acknowledge that he returned to Spain with Native Americans who were pressed into slavery. Despite these facts, Columbus Day should keep its name and continue to celebrate its namesake. Columbus put his own life in jeopardy to travel across the world and discover new sea routes. We laud his role in connecting America and Europe and in taking his European culture to new places. The world would not have flourished as it has if Columbus had not bravely set out to explore new places.

**ARGUMENT** What is the argument of the "Con" passage?

_____

_____

_____

**PERSUASIVE TECHNIQUE** Has the author successfully refuted the opposing viewpoint? Explain.

_____

_____

_____

**ELABORATE KEY IDEAS** Circle two sentences that are effective in elaborating and developing the position in the "Con" passage.

**AUTHOR'S PURPOSE**
What is the author's purpose in writing the "Pro" passage?

_____

_____

**POINT OF VIEW** What is the point of view of the author of the "Pro" passage? Explain.

_____

_____

**EVIDENCE AND INFERENCES** Based on information in the "Pro" passage, what can you infer would be a new name the author would like to see for Columbus Day?

_____

_____

**CENTRAL IDEA** What is the central idea of "Should Columbus Day Be Renamed?"?

_____

_____

**The topic:** The name of Columbus Day should be changed.

**<u>Pro:</u>**

10      Columbus Day's name should be changed because it is a travesty to continue celebrating Christopher Columbus's "achievements" and maintaining the name of the holiday. Our reasons for our position are as follows:

- Columbus and those who followed his path of travel unknowingly brought diseases and caused destruction to the native people who were already living here.

- Giving Columbus credit for discovering America invalidates the fact that native peoples already lived on the land. Columbus could not have "discovered" a land that already served as a home to others—the native peoples.

- Other explorers have been denied recognition for having discovered America. For example, Leif Ericson sailed to North America centuries before Columbus made his voyage.

- Bjarni Herjólfsson is believed to be the first explorer to have laid eyes on America.

What sorts of names have been proposed to rename Columbus Day? Some of these renamings have already been implemented in cities or on college campuses around the country. They include _Discoverers' Day_, _Native American Day_, and _Indigenous_[1] _Peoples Day_.

. . .

As you weigh the pros and cons, consider what you've learned about Columbus and the holiday that honors him. Then consider this: the argument is certain to continue to heat up debates across the nation. What history teaches us is that there are two or more sides in every debate, and that facts may emerge over time that strengthen one argument or another.

[1]**indigenous** native

_Leif Ericson_

_Bjarni Herjólfsson_

## Anchor Standard Discussion Questions

Discuss the following questions with your peer group. Then record your answers in the space provided.

1. In the concluding paragraph of the Columbus Day "Pro" passage, the author makes the point that "facts may emerge over time that strengthen one argument or another." How does this sentence relate to the rest of the argument? What's the author's reason for including it?

_____

_____

_____

_____

_____

_____

2. Choose a claim from either side of the Columbus Day argument that has faulty reasoning or insufficient evidence. Explain why you think the claim is unconvincing. Then suggest ways that the author might strengthen the claim.

_____

_____

_____

_____

_____

## Comprehension Check

1. In the "Con" argument from "Should Columbus Day Be Renamed?" which claim do you think is strongest? Explain.

_____

_____

_____

2. In the "Pro" argument from "Should Columbus Day Be Renamed?" the author includes negative comments regarding Columbus. Was this an effective way of approaching the argument? Use examples from the passage as you explain.

_____

_____

3. Regardless of your personal belief, state which argument regarding Columbus Day— "Pro" or "Con"—is stronger. Explain your answer and include specific examples from the passage in your response.

_____

_____

_____

## Read On Your Own

Read another persuasive nonfiction text, "Fair Pay for Fair Play," independently. Apply what you learned in this lesson and check your understanding.

# Writing Opinion Pieces

**Does your state** use Daylight Savings Time (DST)? During DST, we turn the clocks ahead one hour in the spring. So, 6 a.m. becomes 7 a.m., requiring us to get up earlier. However, 5 p.m. becomes 6 p.m., so we have more daylight for evening activities. Some people love this time of the year and are glad for that extra hour of daylight. Other people, however, think it just complicates our lives. What do you think? Is Daylight Savings Time a good idea or a "waste of time"? You can share your thinking about this issue—and other issues—by writing an opinion piece.

## ESSENTIAL QUESTION

*How can persuasive writing be used effectively to encourage others to support your opinion?*

# What's an Opinion Piece?

Whether you are for or against Daylight Savings Time or another issue, you can share your opinion with others. People have different opinions and don't always agree on an issue. You can write an opinion piece to persuade readers to agree with you.

In an **opinion piece**, you explain what you think about an issue. Then you offer reasons to support your opinion (or argument) and evidence to back up your reasons.

The graphic organizer below shows how to organize an effective opinion piece.

**Introduction**
Introduce the topic in an interesting way. State your opinion/argument about the topic clearly. Tell your readers what you think about the topic.

**Supporting Reasons**
Give at least three clear reasons to support your opinion/argument. Use facts and experiences that support it. The stronger your reasons, the stronger your argument will be.

**Conclusion**
Summarize your opinion/argument and the reasons that support it.

Let's look at an opinion piece.

## Analyze a Mentor Text

This is an example of an effective opinion piece by a sixth grader. Read it and then complete the activities in the boxes as a class.

### Down with DST!

Do we really need a reason to get up earlier? That is what happens every year when Daylight Savings Time, or DST, begins. One Sunday in March, we set all of our clocks ahead one hour. If you usually get up at 6 a.m., now you are getting up at 5 a.m.! The change in time also means one more hour of daylight at the end of the day. In my opinion, we should stop having DST because we have to get up too early, we do not need another hour of daylight in the evening, and the change in time upsets everyone's schedules.

Students are not the only ones who get sleepy when DST starts. Daylight Savings Time affects everyone who lives where it is observed. When DST starts, it is still dark outside, even at 7 a.m. It takes several more weeks before the sun rises between 6 and 7 a.m. We are getting up in the dark, sleepy and irritable just because it is DST.

We do not need that extra hour of daylight in the evening either. Initially, the goal of DST was to save energy. Since we have another hour of daylight, we turn on our lights an hour later every day. That way, we use less electricity. However, we have to turn on our lights an hour earlier on those dark (and cold) mornings. In addition, it is still light at 9 p.m. in the summer, which should be enough daylight for anyone. By 9 p.m., many children head to bed, but who wants to go to bed when it is still light outside? Children are confused; they do not understand why they are going to bed when it is light out, and they often put up a fight. If it were dark out, though, they would not argue.

**STATE AN OPINION/ ARGUMENT**  By asking an interesting question, the writer grabs the reader's attention in the introduction. After stating some facts, the writer clearly states an opinion. Finally, the writer lists the three reasons that will be used to support this opinion. Underline the writer's opinion.

**SUPPORTING REASONS** The writer expands on the reasons for her opinion in the second, third, and fourth paragraphs. Underline the reason stated in each of paragraphs 2 through 4.

**CONCLUSION** This conclusion restates the argument or opinion of the writer and then summarizes the reasons that support it. Draw a box around the opinion stated in this conclusion.

When DST begins, the time change upsets more than our sleeping schedules. How many people are late to religious services, games, practices, and other regularly scheduled events on the day when DST begins? Daylight Savings Time also complicates plane, bus, and train schedules. To make things more confusing, the United States covers six time zones, if you include Alaska and Hawaii. However, Hawaii and parts of Arizona do not follow DST. If you are flying out of an Arizona airport at 1:15 p.m. in the summer, you had better verify that time. Is it Mountain Standard Time? Is it DST?

In conclusion, the termination of DST is long overdue. Daylight Savings Time just makes life more difficult by robbing us of sleep, adding an unneeded hour of daylight in the evening, and complicating our schedules. Maybe DST helped reduce the use of electricity long ago. However, times have changed. Now it is time to terminate DST and make it history.

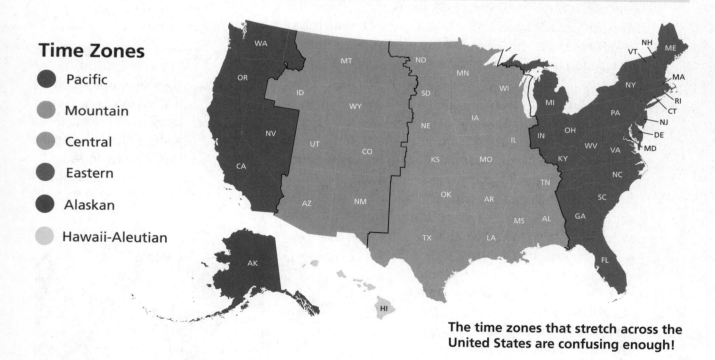

## Time Zones

- Pacific
- Mountain
- Central
- Eastern
- Alaskan
- Hawaii-Aleutian

The time zones that stretch across the United States are confusing enough!

**Think About It ▶** Which reason in this opinion piece do you think was the strongest?

Were you convinced that DST needs to be eliminated? Why or why not?

# Vocabulary Study: Word Roots

Word parts can often provide clues about the meaning of a word. A **root** is the part of a word that carries its core meaning. Many roots come from Greek and Latin words. When you know the meaning of a root, you can use it and the context of the sentence to figure out the meaning of an unfamiliar word.

Here are some common roots. Work with classmates or a partner to fill in the chart.

| Word Parts and Meanings | Example | Meaning |
|---|---|---|
| *geo* means "earth" | geology | study of the earth |
| *term* means "to end" | terminal | |
| *ver* means "truth" | verdict | |
| *chrono* means "time" | chronology | |
| *serv* means "keep, save" | preserve | |

Look back at the opinion piece on pages 197–198. Find three words, each of which uses one of the roots in the chart. Write each word and its meaning in the left column of the chart. Then write a sentence for each word in the right column. Use context clues to suggest each word's meaning.

| | |
|---|---|
| **Word with root:** <br><br> **Word meaning:** | **Sentence:** |
| **Word with root:** <br><br> **Word meaning:** | **Sentence:** |
| **Word with root:** <br><br> **Word meaning:** | **Sentence:** |

# Writing Process

Now that you have read and analyzed an opinion piece, you are going to create your own by following the steps in the writing process.

**1.** **Get Ready: Brainstorm** List topics you want to write about. Choose the one that you have the strongest opinion about. Think of reasons to support your view. Choose the strongest reasons to use in your opinion piece.

**2.** **Organize** Use a graphic organizer to organize supporting details and plan your opinion piece.

**3.** **Draft** Create the first draft of your opinion piece.

**4.** **Peer Review** Work with a partner to evaluate and improve your draft.

**5.** **Revise** Use suggestions from your peer review to revise your opinion piece.

**6.** **Edit** Check your work carefully for errors in spelling, punctuation, and grammar.

**7.** **Publish** Create a final version of your opinion piece.

## Writing Assignment

In this lesson, you will write your own opinion piece. As you create the piece, remember the elements of the mentor text that were most effective. Read the following assignment.

> Should the school day be changed to start later and end later? Decide whether or not you think this would be a good idea. Then write an opinion piece of at least five paragraphs that explains and supports your opinion.

# 1. Get Ready: Brainstorm

The first step in writing your opinion piece is refining your assigned topic. Begin by thinking about positive and negative aspects of starting the school day later. For each one, think about how you feel about changing the time school begins.

Here's how the writer of the mentor opinion piece brainstormed opinions.

| Opinion | Positive Aspects | Negative Aspects |
|---|---|---|
| DST should end. | We would not have to change the clocks or get used to a different schedule twice a year. | We would not have much daylight after school in the spring. |
| DST should continue. | We could keep doing what we always do. In the spring, we would have more daylight after school. | It is hard to get used to a new schedule twice a year. People end up being early or late on those days. |

## Try It! Use a Brainstorming Graphic Organizer

Now use the chart below to help brainstorm your own opinions about whether the school day should start and end later. Choose the argument that you feel is stronger.

| Opinion | Positive Aspects | Negative Aspects |
|---|---|---|
| | | |
| | | |

# Brainstorm Ideas for Your Topic

You can use a graphic organizer to help brainstorm ideas and details to support your opinion piece. Here is how the writer of the mentor text used a graphic organizer.

**OPINION/ ARGUMENT** Begin by stating your opinion clearly and strongly.

**REASONS** Give three clear reasons that support your opinion or argument. As you draft your opinion piece, you might add to or revise your reasons.

**SUPPORT** Support your reasons with facts and your own experiences. You will probably think of more details to include as you draft your opinion piece.

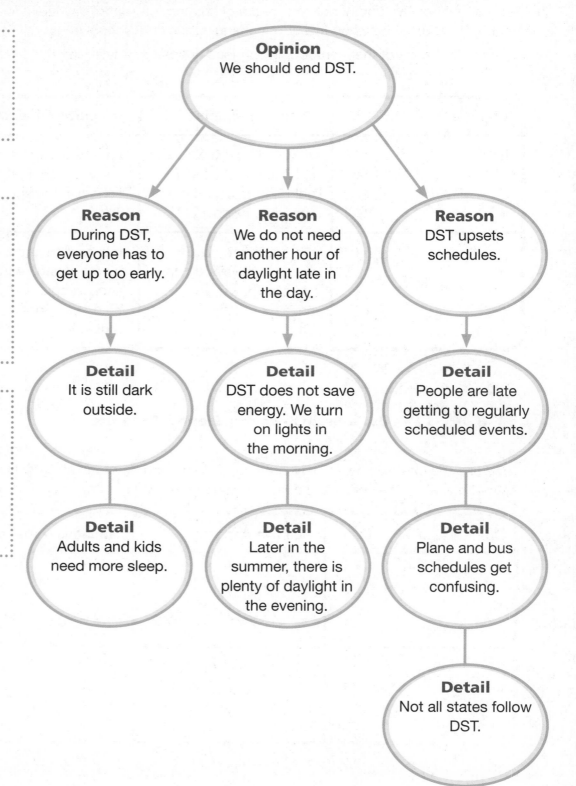

**Opinion**
We should end DST.

**Reason**
During DST, everyone has to get up too early.

**Reason**
We do not need another hour of daylight late in the day.

**Reason**
DST upsets schedules.

**Detail**
It is still dark outside.

**Detail**
DST does not save energy. We turn on lights in the morning.

**Detail**
People are late getting to regularly scheduled events.

**Detail**
Adults and kids need more sleep.

**Detail**
Later in the summer, there is plenty of daylight in the evening.

**Detail**
Plane and bus schedules get confusing.

**Detail**
Not all states follow DST.

# Try It!    Use a Graphic Organizer for Brainstorming

You can use a graphic organizer to brainstorm your opinion, reasons, and supporting details for your opinion piece.

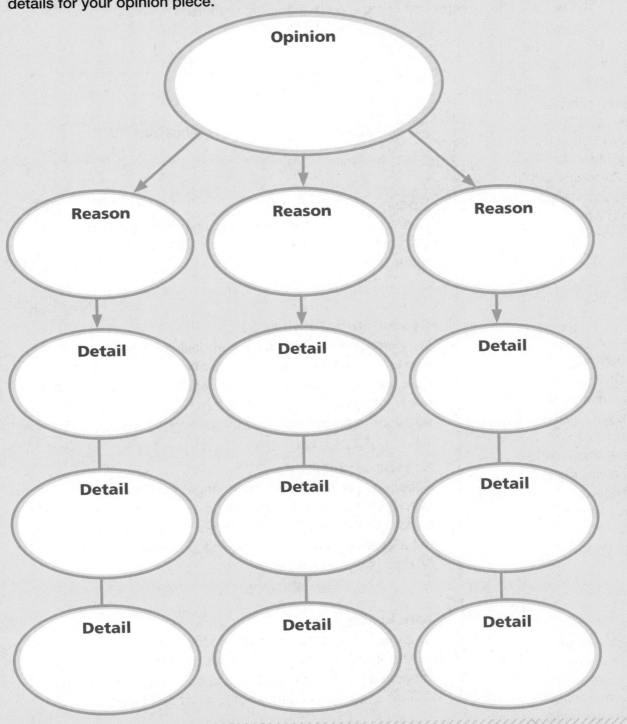

# 2. Organize

You are almost ready to begin a draft of your opinion piece. You can use a graphic organizer to organize the reasons and support that you gathered during brainstorming. You can refer to the graphic organizer as you work through different parts of your draft. The writer of the mentor text completed this graphic organizer.

**INTRODUCTION** In the first paragraph, you introduce the topic and state your opinion about the topic. The mentor text writer also reviewed how DST works, in case readers were unclear about it.

**SUPPORTING PARAGRAPHS** The next paragraphs give reasons to support your opinion. They also offer facts, details, and personal experiences to support your reasons.

**CONCLUSION** In the final paragraph, you restate your opinion, summarize your reasons, and appeal to your reader.

**Opinion**
We should stop using Daylight Savings Time (DST).

**Reason and Details**
Everyone has to start getting up an hour earlier, and it is still dark out for a month or more after DST starts. We all need more sleep.

**Reason and Details**
We do not need an extra hour of daylight in the evening. Any energy we save is used up when we turn on lights an hour earlier in the morning. Besides, by the time summer starts, we have daylight until 9 p.m.—long enough. Kids do not want to go to bed when it is still light outside.

**Reason and Details**
People forget about the time change and are late to everything that first day. Plus, bus and plane schedules become confusing. The time zones cause enough confusion, but it gets worse during DST because not all states use it. Arizona is one example.

**Conclusion**
I hope you agree that we should stop using DST, as it just makes life more difficult. It robs us of sleep, adds an unneeded hour of daylight, and upsets schedules. Maybe DST was helpful long ago, but it is not helpful now.

# Try It!

**Organize Your Opinion Piece**

Now use the graphic organizer below to organize the ideas and details you want to use in the different paragraphs of your draft.

**Opinion**

**Reason 1 and Details**

**Reason 2 and Details**

**Reason 3 and Details**

**Conclusion**

# 3. Draft

Next, you will write the draft of your opinion piece. Remember, a draft is not meant to be perfect. The goal is just to get your ideas on paper. This is the time to use your notes, get your ideas down in an organized way, and experiment with different ways to present your argument effectively. You will have time to revise your writing later.

## Writer's Craft: Using Relationships Between Ideas

As you draft and later revise your opinion piece, you need to show how your ideas are connected. You can do this by using transition words and phrases to show clear relationship between ideas.

Here are some common transition words and phrases.

| | |
|---|---|
| **Transition words** | however, so, if, then, since, because, but, initially, so, later, during |
| **Transition phrases** | in addition, that way, as long as, in fact, in the same way, as a result |

The writer of the mentor text uses transition words and phrases in the third paragraph.

**TRANSITION WORDS** Read this section of the mentor text. Circle the transition words the writer uses. Then underline the transition phrases the writer uses.

We do not need that extra hour of daylight in the evening either. Initially, the goal of DST was to save energy. Since we have another hour of daylight, we turn on our lights an hour later every day. That way, we use less electricity. However, we have to turn on our lights an hour earlier on those dark (and cold) mornings. In addition, it is still light at 9 p.m. in the summer, which should be enough daylight for anyone. By 9 p.m., many children head to bed, but who wants to go to bed when it is still light outside?

# Try It!

**Write Your First Draft**

On a computer or on a separate sheet of paper, create the draft of your opinion piece. Remember to use words, phrases, or clauses to show clear relationships between the ideas. Use this drafting checklist to help you as you write.

✓ Use the introduction to grab your reader's attention. You might begin with a question, quotation, or funny experience.

✓ State your opinion in the first paragraph.

✓ Begin each supporting paragraph with a topic sentence that states a reason that supports your opinion or argument.

✓ Use the reasons and support from your graphic organizer.

✓ In each supporting paragraph, include sentences with details, facts, and experiences.

✓ In the conclusion, restate your opinion and summarize the reasons that support your argument.

## Tips for Writing Your First Draft

- Discuss your topic—and your opinion about it—with friends and family members. Other people might offer new reasons to support your opinion.

- Do not stop to check spelling or worry about punctuation or grammar. You will have time for that later, when you revise and edit.

- If you are having trouble getting started on your draft, pretend that you are explaining your ideas to a friend. Then write down what you say.

# 4. Peer Review

After you finish your draft, you can work with a partner to review each other's drafts. Here is a draft of the mentor text. Read it with your partner. Together, answer the questions in the boxes. On the next page, you will read how the mentor text writer's partner reviewed the draft.

**INTRODUCTION**
The writer states an opinion and gives three reasons. How could the writer grab the reader's attention? How could the writer combine sentences 2 and 3 to show how those ideas are related?

**SUPPORTING PARAGRAPHS**
In paragraph 3, the writer states that DST doesn't save energy, but she doesn't provide evidence to support this statement. How could you combine two sentences to show how the ideas are connected?

**CONCLUSION** This conclusion restates the writer's opinion and sums up the reasons. How could the writer encourage readers to agree with the opinion?

## Down with DST!

One Sunday in March, we set all of our clocks ahead one hour. Let's say you usually get up at 6 a.m. Now you are getting up at 5 a.m.! There is also one more hour of daylight at the end of the day. We should stop having DST because we have to get up too early, we do not need another hour of daylight in the evening, and the change in time upsets everyone's schedules.

Not just students get sleepy when DST starts, you know. Everyone has to start getting up an hour earlier. Adults and kids need more sleep than they get. When DST starts, it is still dark outside at 6 or even 7 a.m. We're still getting up in the dark, even though it's DST. What gives?

We do not need that extra hour of daylight in the evening. It was supposed to save energy. It doesn't. In addition, it's still light at 9 p.m. in the summer, which is enough daylight for anyone! By 9 p.m., it's time for most children to go to bed. No one wants to go to bed when it's still light outside. If it were dark out, though, they would not argue.

When DST begins, the time change makes people late for religious services, sports games, birthday parties, and other events. DST also complicates plane, bus, and train schedules. The United States covers six time zones, so that is confusing enough. To make it worse, Hawaii and parts of Arizona do not follow DST. If you're flying out of an Arizona airport at 1:15 p.m. in the summer, you had better verify the time. Is it Mountain Standard Time? Is it DST?

The termination of DST is overdue. It just makes life more difficult by robbing us of sleep, adding an unneeded hour of daylight in the evening, and confusing schedules. Maybe DST helped long ago, when people used lanterns for light. However, now it's time to get rid of DST!

# An Example Peer Review Form

This peer review form shows how a partner evaluated the draft of the mentor text on the previous page.

| | |
|---|---|
| **The first paragraph introduces the topic in an interesting way.** | You did a good job of stating your opinion and the three reasons that support it. |
| **The writer clearly states an opinion about the topic.** | You could improve your opinion piece by grabbing the reader's attention more effectively. Think about how DST affects your reader. |

| | |
|---|---|
| **The writer supports the opinion with at least three strong reasons.** | You did a good job of giving three strong reasons. |
| **The writer uses interesting details, facts, and experiences to explain the reasons.** | You could improve your opinion piece by adding more details about your reasons. |

| | |
|---|---|
| **The writer shows the connections between ideas.** | You did a good job of using "in addition" in your third paragraph to show that you are moving on to a new, related idea. |
| | You could improve your opinion piece by combining more words, phrases, and clauses to show how the ideas relate to each other. |

| | |
|---|---|
| **The conclusion restates the opinion and summarizes the reasons and supporting details.** | You did a good job of restating your opinion and summing up your reasons. |
| **The writer appeals to the reader.** | You could improve your opinion piece by appealing to the reader or inviting the reader to agree with you. |

# Try It!

**Peer Review with a Partner**

Now you are going to work with a partner to review each other's opinion piece drafts. You will use the peer review form below. If you need help, look back at the mentor text writer's peer review form for suggestions.

| | |
|---|---|
| **The first paragraph introduces the topic in an interesting way.**<br><br>**The writer clearly states an opinion about the topic.** | You did a good job of<br><br>You could improve your opinion piece by |
| **The writer supports the opinion with at least three strong reasons.**<br><br>**The writer uses interesting details, facts, and experiences to explain the reasons.** | You did a good job of<br><br>You could improve your opinion piece by |
| **The writer shows the connections between ideas.** | You did a good job of<br><br>You could improve your opinion piece by |
| **The conclusion restates the opinion and summarizes the reasons and supporting details.**<br><br>**The writer appeals to the reader.** | You did a good job of<br><br>You could improve your opinion piece by |

# Try It!

**Record Key Peer Review Comments**

Now it is time for you and your partner to share your comments with each other. Listen to your partner's feedback, and write down the key comments in the left column. Then write some ideas for improving your draft in the right column.

| | |
|---|---|
| My reviewer says that my introduction | I will |
| My reviewer says that my first supporting reason | I will |
| My reviewer says that my second supporting reason | I will |
| My reviewer says that my third supporting reason | I will |
| My reviewer says that my conclusion | I will |

Write anything else you notice about your draft that you think you can improve.

# 5. Revise

In this step of the writing process, you will use your own ideas and your partner's feedback to strengthen your draft. Use this checklist as you revise.

**Revision Checklist**

✔ Does my introduction grab the reader's interest? Do I state my topic and opinion clearly?

✔ Are all of my reasons important? Do they support my opinion in a strong way?

✔ Do I use details, facts, and experiences to make my reasons clear and strong?

✔ Is my conclusion interesting? Have I summed up my opinion and reasons well? Do I appeal to the reader or invite the reader to agree with me?

✔ Do I use words, phrases, and clauses to connect my ideas?

✔ Do I use formal language in my opinion piece?

**FORMAL LANGUAGE**

Formal language is a style of writing used for reports and essays. It makes your opinion piece seem polished and professional. How would the paragraph sound if the writer used the word *kids* instead of *students* and the word *grouchy* instead of *irritable*?

_____

_____

## Writer's Craft: Using Formal Language

Formal language makes you seem like an expert on the topic. Informal language includes slang and words used with friends. To use formal language:

- Do not use phrases such as *you know*, *like I said*, or *anyway*.
- Avoid starting sentences with *and*, *but*, or *so*.
- Use exclamation points sparingly.
- Avoid contractions and write out words: *you would*, not *you'd*.
- Substitute more formal words for words such as *kids*.

The writer of the mentor text used formal language below.

> Students are not the only ones who get sleepy when DST starts. Daylight Savings Time affects everyone who lives where it is observed. When DST starts, it is still dark outside, even at 7 a.m. It takes several more weeks before the sun rises between 6 and 7 a.m. We are getting up in the dark, sleepy and irritable just because it is DST.

# Try It! Revise Your Opinion Piece

Replacing informal language with formal language is part of revising an opinion piece. In the paragraph, replace each underlined word/phrase with a formal word/phrase or write D to delete the word/phrase.

Experts <u>aren't</u> sure whether DST saves energy. During spring, we have to turn on the lights an hour earlier, <u>you know</u>, which cancels out any savings when we turn on the lights an hour later in the evening. <u>Anyway</u>, it wastes a <u>ton</u> of time to change all those clocks. One study estimates that it costs over $800,000 to set our clocks ahead. <u>And</u> then we set them back again in the fall. <u>Can you believe that?</u> <u>What a waste!</u>

Replace *aren't* with _____

Replace *you know* with _____

Replace *Anyway* with _____

Replace *ton* with _____

Replace *And* with _____

Replace *Can you believe that?* with _____

Replace *What a waste!* with _____

## Writing Assignment

Continue working on a computer or on a separate sheet of paper. Review the assignment and the checklist so know you have included everything.

> Should the school day be changed to start later and end later? Decide whether or not you think this would be a good idea. Then write an opinion piece of at least five paragraphs that explains and supports your opinion.

# 6. Edit

The next step in revising your opinion piece is to edit it. You will read it very carefully to identify and fix any mistakes. Here's a checklist of things to look for.

**Editing Checklist**

✔ Did you indent each paragraph?

✔ Are all of your sentences complete? Does each have a subject and a verb?

✔ Did you begin each sentence with a capital letter?

✔ Does each sentence end with the correct punctuation?

✔ Have you used commas and parentheses correctly?

✔ Are all of your words spelled correctly?

You can use these editing marks to mark any errors you find.

| | | |
|---|---|---|
| ^ Insert | ⊙ Insert period | ⟋ Delete |
| ⸲ Insert comma | ∩ Reverse order | ⟨⟩ Insert parentheses |
| ◡ Close up space | # Add space | ⌐ Indent |

This paragraph from an earlier draft of the mentor text shows how to use editing marks.

⌐The termination of DST is overdue. It just makes life more difficult by robbing us of sleep, adding an unneeded hour of day light in the evening, and confusing schedules. Maybe DST helped long ago, when people used lanterns for light. However, now it is time to get rid of Daylight Savings Time!

# Language Focus: Using Commas and Parentheses

You can use **commas** or **parentheses** to set off a phrase or clause that is not essential to the meaning of a sentence. Compare these two examples:

> Jen shared her sandwich with Jeff, <u>who forgot his lunch today</u>.

The underlined clause is not essential in this sentence. We know who Jeff is because he is named.

> Jen shared her sandwich with a friend <u>who forgot his lunch today</u>.

Here, the underlined clause is essential to the meaning of the sentence. Without this clause, we don't know with whom Jen shared her sandwich.

You can also use parentheses to set off nonessential information, like in this example:

> Peg headed for the house on the corner (the one with the red door).

The information enclosed in parentheses is extra, not essential. Instead of using parentheses, you could use a comma after *corner* in order to show a pause.

We do not need that extra hour of daylight in the evening either. Initially, the goal of DST was to save energy. Since we have another hour of daylight, we turn on our lights an hour later every day. That way, we use less electricity. However, we have to turn on our lights an hour earlier on those dark (and cold) mornings. In addition, it is still light at 9 p.m. in the summer, which should be enough daylight for anyone. By 9 p.m., many children head to bed, but who wants to go to bed when it is still light outside? Children are confused; they do not understand why they are going to bed when it is light out, and they often put up a fight. If it were dark out, though, they would not argue.

**COMMAS AND PARENTHESES**
Read this section of the mentor text. Underline the nonessential clause set off by a comma and the nonessential words set off by parentheses in this paragraph.

# Try It!

**Language and Editing Practice**

Read each sentence. Rewrite sentences that need commas or parentheses.

1. This is my sister Jen who plays on the school basketball team.

   _____

2. The book the one that I lost belongs to the library.

   _____

3. Before I ate my lunch I bought milk at the store that is on the corner.

   _____

4. Mr. Wilson who is our track coach was given an award for service.

   _____

5. The girl who is sitting next to Kim is my neighbor Jessie.

   _____

Now use editing marks to correct the errors in this paragraph.

Can you beleive that massive thunderstorm last night? All of the lightning

thunder and rain kept me awake until dawn or maybe it was more like a couple

of hours. Then our electricity goes out. When my dog jumped onto my bed and

I nearly hit the ceiling.

# Try It!

**Edit Your Opinion Piece**

Now edit your opinion piece. Use this checklist and the editing marks you have learned to correct any errors you find.

- ☐ Have you indented each paragraph?

- ☐ Are all of your sentences complete? Does each have a subject and a verb?

- ☐ Did you begin each sentence with a capital letter?

- ☐ Does each sentence end with the correct punctuation?

- ☐ Have you used commas and parentheses correctly?

- ☐ Are all of your words spelled correctly?

- ☐ Do you make clear relationships among ideas?

- ☐ Have you used formal language?

## Editing Tips

- Ask a friend or family member to read your opinion piece aloud. Take notes as you listen for awkward phrases, missing words, or repeated ideas.

- Read your writing backward, word for word, starting at the end. You will be more likely to spot spelling mistakes this way.

- Review when it is appropriate to use commas and parentheses. Reread your writing to make sure punctuation has been used correctly.

- Put your writing aside and do something else, at least for a few minutes. Even getting up to sharpen your pencil can help clear your mind. Then you will be able to find errors that tired eyes might overlook.

# 7. Publish

On a computer or a separate sheet of paper, create a neat final draft of your opinion piece. Correct all of the errors that you identified while editing your draft. Be sure to give your opinion piece an interesting title.

The final step is to publish your opinion piece. Here are some ways you might share your work:

- Create a poster with your opinion piece using graphics of clocks, the rising/setting sun, or other images related to your topic.

- Display the class's opinion pieces on a bulletin board in the school hallway under the heading *For* or *Against*. Add a title that explains the topic.

- Submit your opinion piece to your school newspaper as a letter to the editor.

- Read your opinion piece aloud in a small group that includes classmates who have different opinions about the topic. Try to persuade others to agree with you.

### Technology Suggestions
- Upload your opinion piece to a class or school blog.
- Use eye-catching shapes, colors, fonts, or clip art to create the poster described above.

# Writing Handbook

## A Guide to Functional Texts

Functional texts are things you read and write to help you in your day-to-day life. If you need to cook something, you read the recipe first. If you are going to a special event, you read the invitation to find out when and where the event will be. If you invite a friend to your house, you may need to write directions and include a map. In this section, you will find examples of different functional texts and labels that show you the important features of each text. If you are asked to read or write one of these functional texts, use the sample in this handbook as a model to follow.

Write the sender's name and address in the upper-left corner. Be sure to include the city, state, and zip code.

Stamps go in the upper-right corner.

Sender's Name
Street Address
City, State Zip Code

Recipient's Name
Street Address
City, State Zip Code

The name and address of the person getting the letter should be in the center. Be sure to include the city, state, and zip code.

Scott Mester
12 White Knoll Drive
Pleasantville, NY 12345

Carolyn Long
34 Church Road
Old Bridge, Michigan 45678

Your address should be given at the top of the letter.

Include the address of the person to whom you are sending the letter.

Include the date.

Address the person you are writing with a formal greeting, including any appropriate titles such as "Mr." or "Ms."

347 Elm Street
Baton Rouge, LA 70801

March 4, 2012

Mr. Frederick Wright
959 Canal Street
New Orleans, LA 70111

Dear Mr. Wright:

The body paragraphs of your letter should be well organized and clear. Be sure to maintain a formal tone.

Thank you for responding to my letter. I have not had a chance to read your new book. It will have to wait until school is over. Thank you for answering my questions. Your answers were very helpful. I received an "A" on my assignment. My teacher said she was impressed. She had never seen so many facts and information about your book.

My new assignment is about jungle cats. My teacher gave us a list of topics to research. I chose jungle cats. I read different sources in the library. They gave me a lot of information about jungle cats. You mentioned that you went to Africa in your last letter. Did you see any jungle cats?

Sincerely,

*Andrew Walker*
Andrew Walker

Remember that your closing should match the overall tone of the rest of the letter. "Regards" and "Sincerely" are good choices.

Sign your letter. Under your signature, type your first and last name so there will be no confusion about the spelling of your name.

Start by giving the reason for the event and inviting your guests to attend.

**Brooke Edwards is celebrating her thirteenth birthday!**

\* 13 \*

Join us as we celebrate on
Saturday, May 19, 2012 at 5:00 p.m.

Include the date and time of the event.

Northern Ice Skating Rink
123 N. Sunrise Highway
Middletown, Virginia

Provide the location's name and address.

Regrets only to Mr. and Mrs. Edwards (123) 456-7890.

Provide a way for your guests to respond to the invitation.

Address the person you are writing to with a standard greeting. You may choose to include titles or address them as "Mr." or "Ms."

Dear Aunt Ruth,

    Thank you for the sweater you sent for my birthday. You have always understood my taste in clothes, and it is just what I needed now that the weather has changed.

    I hope you and Uncle Hank are well, and I look forward to seeing you at Christmas.

With love,

*Billy*

The body paragraphs of your letter should be well organized and clear.

The length should be short.

Your closing should match the tone of the rest of the letter. "With thanks" and "Best" are good choices.

Sign your note.

Place a photo in your report or presentation. Use a photo that shows something your readers might not have seen before.

The caption should be directly below the photo.

**Buffalo are usually brown. White buffalo are very rare and are considered sacred by some Native American groups.**

Be sure to say exactly what is in the photo. You may provide extra information that relates to the report.

Decide what information you want to show and divide the chart into columns.

A heading should be at the top of each column.

| Context Clue Type | Example |
|---|---|
| Definition | We can learn about dinosaurs through *paleontology, the study of fossils*. |
| Synonym | In many ways, early *littoral* settlements in Ireland resembled the *coastal* villages there today. |
| Contrast | We expected the hotel to be *opulent*, but instead we found *cracked ceilings*, *leaky faucets*, and *cramped, run-down rooms*. |
| Association | Betsey's bedroom was in complete *chaos. Piles of clothes* lay *all over the floor, books and papers* were *spilling off the desk*, and a *half-eaten pizza* poked out from *under the bed*. |

List items under the first column so they start their own row.

Items in the next column should relate to the heading and the item at the left in that row.

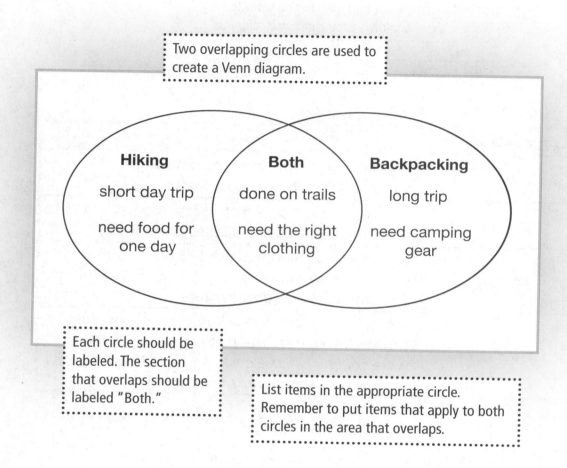

Two overlapping circles are used to create a Venn diagram.

**Hiking**

short day trip

need food for one day

**Both**

done on trails

need the right clothing

**Backpacking**

long trip

need camping gear

Each circle should be labeled. The section that overlaps should be labeled "Both."

List items in the appropriate circle. Remember to put items that apply to both circles in the area that overlaps.

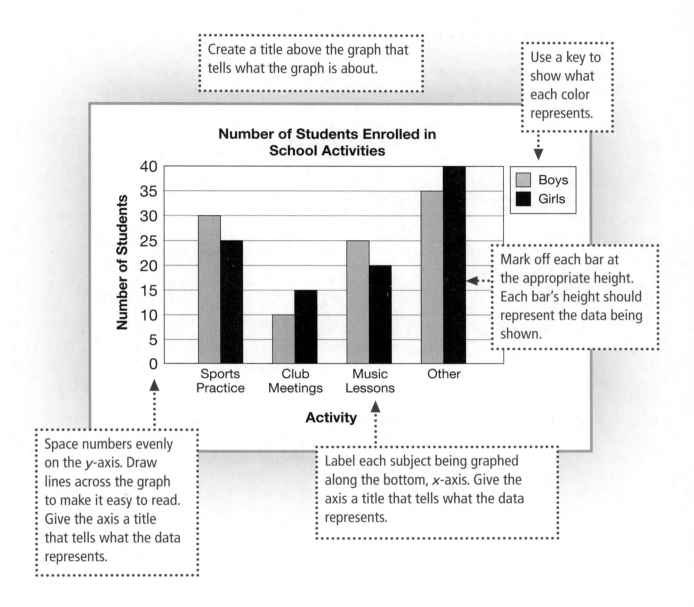

Create a title above the graph that tells what the graph is about.

Use a key to show what each color represents.

**Number of Students Enrolled in School Activities**

Boys
Girls

Mark off each bar at the appropriate height. Each bar's height should represent the data being shown.

Space numbers evenly on the *y*-axis. Draw lines across the graph to make it easy to read. Give the axis a title that tells what the data represents.

Label each subject being graphed along the bottom, *x*-axis. Give the axis a title that tells what the data represents.

Label the area that the map represents.

Label relevant regions, cities, rivers, bodies of water, and landmarks.

Show important boundaries.

## Texas Chili

**Ingredients:**

- 1 lb beef, cubed
- ½ cup beef broth
- ½ cup chicken broth
- 1 cup chopped tomatoes
- 3 serrano peppers
- 1 tsp onion powder
- 1 tsp garlic powder
- 1½ Tbsp chili powder
- salt

> The name of the dish should be given at the top of the page.

> List all the ingredients needed for the recipe.

> Include measurements of ingredients.

> Directions should be listed and numbered.

**Directions:**

1. Brown the beef in a pan over medium heat.

2. Drain the beef, and set it aside.

3. Bring the beef broth, chicken broth, and tomatoes to a boil in a pot.

4. Add the serrano peppers, onion powder, garlic powder, chili powder, and a pinch of salt.

5. Add the beef, and simmer for about 60 minutes over medium-low heat.

> Instructions should be written clearly. Be sure they explain all the steps necessary to make the dish.

> Be sure to provide cooking time.

Title the procedure.

# How to Make a Bolo Tie

**Supplies**

- leather strip (30 to 40 inches long)
- strong safety pin
- something decorative but not too large, such as a wooden button or an old belt buckle
- beads
- strong glue

List all the materials needed.

- scissors

**Instructions**

**Step 1:** Place the leather strip around your neck. Ask yourself: Is the strip the length I want it to be? If the strip is too long for your liking, use the scissors to trim it.

**Step 2:** Decorate both ends of the leather strip with beads. If your beads have large enough holes, slide them over each end, and tie the ends of the strip to keep the beads in place. If your beads are too small, dip each end of the leather strip into glue. Then dip the ends into a pile of the tiny beads so that the ends are covered in beads.

Procedure steps should be numbered.

**Step 3:** Hang the strip in a place where the glue can dry. Be sure the ends of the strip do not touch as they dry.

**Step 4:** Now make the decorative clasp. Your decoration can be a wooden button, an old belt buckle, a plastic flower, or anything you like. Glue the safety pin to the back of the decoration.

**Step 5:** When the leather strip and clasp are both dry, put the strip back around your neck. Carefully guide both pieces of the strip into the safety pin and close the pin. Now you have your own fashionable bolo tie!

Instructions should be written clearly. Be sure they explain exactly what steps must be done and how to complete them.

Title the experiment.

List all the materials needed for the experiment.

Procedure steps should be numbered.

## Static Electricity Experiment

**Materials:**

- a hard rubber or plastic comb
- thread
- pieces of dry, O-shaped cereal

**Procedure:**

1. Tie one piece of cereal to the end of a foot-long piece of thread. You may use any kind of knot you choose.

2. Attach the other end of the thread to something that is not close to anything else so that the piece of cereal is hanging freely.

3. Next, clean the comb well and dry it.

4.  Run the comb through long, dry hair a couple of times or rub the comb on a rug.

5.  Gently and slowly, pass the comb near the cereal. It should move toward the comb to touch it. Hold the comb still until the cereal moves away on its own.

6.  Try to touch the comb to the cereal again. It should move away as the comb comes near.

Read a title at the top of the label.

List all items separately.

If more information is needed, use an asterisk (*) and provide the additional information later.

Remember to keep wording short. Space is limited, so only use the words that are needed.

## Nutrition Facts

Serving Size 8 oz
Servings Per Container  About 3

**Amount Per Serving**

| Calories 180 | Calories from Fat 60 |
|---|---|

| | % Daily Value* |
|---|---|
| **Total Fat** 6g | 10% |
| Saturated Fat 1g | 5% |
| Trans Fat | 0% |
| **Cholesterol**  5mg | 2% |
| **Sodium**  75mg | 3% |
| **Total Carbohydrate**  26g | 9% |
| Dietary Fiber  5g | 19% |
| Sugars  11g | |
| **Protein**  8g | |

| Vitamin A 60% | Vitamin C 70% |
|---|---|
| Calcium  8% | Iron  10% |

*Percent Daily Values are based on a 2,000 calorie diet. Your daily values may be higher or lower depending on your calorie needs.

| | Calories | 2,000 | 2,500 |
|---|---|---|---|
| Total Fat | Less than | 65g | 80g |
| Sat Fat | Less than | 20g | 25g |
| Cholesterol | Less than | 300mg | 300mg |
| Sodium | Less than | 2,400mg | 2,400mg |
| Total Carbohydrate | | 300m | 375g |
| Dietary Fiber | | 25g | 30g |

Calories per gram:

Fat 9          Carbohydrate  4          Protein  4

The title of a time line tells you what subject the time line is explaining.

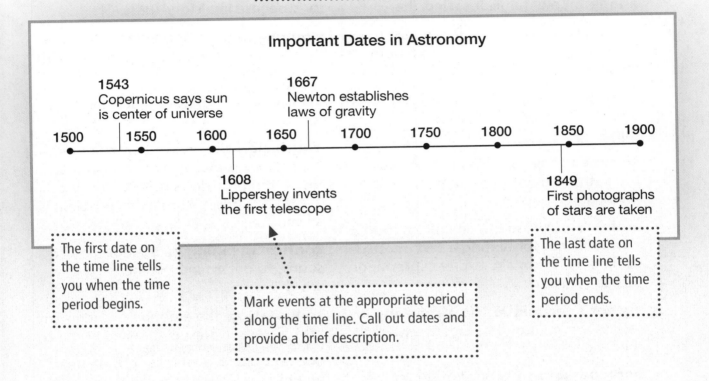

**Important Dates in Astronomy**

**1543**
Copernicus says sun is center of universe

**1667**
Newton establishes laws of gravity

1500  1550  1600  1650  1700  1750  1800  1850  1900

**1608**
Lippershey invents the first telescope

**1849**
First photographs of stars are taken

The first date on the time line tells you when the time period begins.

Mark events at the appropriate period along the time line. Call out dates and provide a brief description.

The last date on the time line tells you when the time period ends.

# Glossary

**academic vocabulary** words used in content-specific areas, such as social studies, mathematics, or science (Lesson 8)

**adage** an old, familiar saying (Lesson 3)

**affix** a letter or letters placed at the beginning or end of a word to modify its meaning (Lessons 4, 7)

**analogy** a comparison that shows a relationship between two sets of things (Lessons 1, 3)

**argument** the central idea that expresses the author's point of view in persuasive nonfiction (Lessons 11, 12)

**author's purpose** the main reason an author has for writing a text, most commonly to explain, express, inform, or persuade (Lessons 7, 11)

**author's technique** the way an author relates information in a creative way to the reader (Lesson 1)

**body paragraph** groups of sentences that provide more information about the central idea (Lessons 2, 8, 12)

**cause** something that brings about an effect or a result (Lesson 1)

**central idea** the most important idea in a text (Lessons 1, 4, 7, 8, 11)

**character** a person, animal, or other creature that takes part in the action of a story or poem (Lessons 3, 5, 6)

**chronology** the time order in which events occur (Lesson 1)

**cite evidence** to point to examples in a text that support the central idea or an inference (Lessons 1, 3, 4)

**claim** a statement a writer makes to support an argument (Lesson 11)

**climax** the moment of greatest tension or suspense in a story (Lesson 5)

**comma** a punctuation mark used most frequently as a mark of separation within a sentence (Lesson 12)

**compare** to look for similarities (Lessons 1, 3)

**conclusion** the end of a piece of writing that sums up the writer's main points and often provides a reflection (Lessons 2, 8, 10, 12); how a conflict or problem is solved (Lessons 5, 10)

**confirm meaning** to use a reference source to determine the meaning of a word (Lesson 3)

**connotation** the emotion or judgment that a word expresses (Lessons 1, 3, 10, 11)

**context clues** a word or phrase near an unknown word that can help the reader determine the unknown word's meaning (Lessons 1, 2, 3, 4, 7)

**contrast** to look for differences (Lesson 3)

**credibility** the reliability of a source used for factual information (Lesson 8)

**denotation** the dictionary definition of a word (Lessons 1, 3, 10)

**dialogue** the words that characters speak in a text; a conversation between characters in a text (Lesson 5)

**effect** the result of a cause (Lesson 1)

**elaborate key ideas** to provide examples and illustrations in support of an argument (Lesson 11)

**elements of drama** the parts of a play, including acts, scenes, stage directions, dialogue, and a cast of characters (Lesson 6)

**evaluate evidence** to assess an author's arguments to see if they are relevant and reliable (Lesson 11)

**evidence** information an author provides to support the central idea of a text, including examples, research and survey results, statistics, case studies, anecdotes, expert opinions, and direct quotations (Lesson 11)

**fact** evidence that helps to convey the main idea of a text (Lesson 8)

**figurative language** a word or phrase that means something other than its dictionary definition, such as a simile, an idiom, a metaphor, or personification (Lessons 1, 3, 6, 9)

**formal language** language that avoids slang in order to convey a professional image; often used in reports and essays (Lesson 12)

**geographic location** the homeland of an author, which can influence his or her perspective (Lesson 3)

**graphic** a chart, graph, map, or diagram that helps the reader understand the text (Lessons 4, 7)

**historical text** a text that includes facts about laws, social customs, and events from the past or current events (Lesson 4)

**inference** an educated guess based on evidence in a text and what you already know (Lessons 1, 3, 6, 9, 11)

**information in art** details that come from a photo or illustration and help the reader understand the text (Lesson 8)

**intensive pronoun** a word that ends in *-self* or *-selves* that emphasizes the noun or nouns it goes with (Lesson 5)

**introduction** the beginning of a piece of writing that captures the reader's attention and sets the scene (Lessons 2, 5, 8, 10, 12)

**linking word** a word that connects ideas (Lesson 10)

**main points** information that supports a thesis (Lesson 10)

**metaphor** a type of figurative language that makes a comparison without using *like* or *as* (Lesson 1)

**narrator** the person who tells a story (Lesson 3)

**object pronoun** a pronoun that acts as an object in a sentence (Lesson 5)

**opinion** a view that someone takes on a certain issue based on a personal judgment (Lesson 12)

**parentheses** punctuation marks that are used to set off a word, phrase, or sentence that is not essential to the meaning of the sentence (Lesson 12)

**personification** a type of figurative language that attributes humanlike qualities to something that is nonhuman (Lesson 1)

**persuasive nonfiction** writing that states an argument in support of a writer's point of view about an issue or topic (Lesson 11)

**persuasive technique** a way in which an author tries to influence the reader's opinion, including bandwagon appeal, name-calling, snob appeal, opposing viewpoints, and stereotyping (Lesson 11)

**plot** the series of related events that build toward the climax of a story (Lessons 3, 5, 6)

**poetic content** the message that a poem sends (often ideas and feelings) (Lesson 9)

**poetry** a literary form, written in verse, that often contains rhyming words (Lesson 9)

**point of view** the perspective from which a story or poem is told, most commonly first person or third person (Lessons 2, 3, 9); the writer's perspective about a topic or issue (Lesson 11)

**possessive pronoun** a pronoun that shows ownership (Lesson 5)

**precise language** words that indicate exactly what the author wishes to convey, bringing images in a text to life (Lesson 2)

**predict word meaning** to look at parts of a word and nearby words to guess the definition of an unknown word (Lessons 1, 3)

**primary source** a document, speech, image, or other piece of evidence created by someone who experienced an event (Lesson 1)

**problem** the conflict in a story that its characters must resolve (Lesson 5)

**pronoun** a word that is used in place of a noun (Lessons 2, 5, 10)

**proverb** an old, familiar saying that conveys wisdom (Lesson 3)

**quotation** the words someone said; usually appear within quotation marks (Lesson 8)

**reference source** a source of information, such as a dictionary, a thesaurus, or a glossary, that can help readers understand a text (Lessons 1, 3, 4)

**relevant details** information in a text that supports the central idea (Lesson 8)

**resolution** in a narrative, the solution to the problem, or the part of the plot that takes place after the climax (Lesson 5)

**rhythm** a repeated pattern of stressed and unstressed syllables (Lesson 9)

**root** the main part of a word (Lessons 4, 7, 12)

**science symbol** a figure or formula used to simplify elements or terms and make them understandable to scientists around the globe (Lesson 7)

**science term** a word or phrase that has a particular meaning in a specific area of scientific study (Lesson 7)

**scientific text** a text that provides facts about living things, nonliving things, Earth and space, and physical properties (Lesson 7)

**secondary source** a work created or written about an event by a person who was not present when the event happened (Lesson 1)

**sensory language** words or phrases that appeal to the reader's sense of sight, hearing, smell, taste, or touch (Lesson 5)

**sentence structure** the length and type of sentences used in a text (Lesson 10)

**setting** where and when a story takes place (Lesson 5)

**simile** a type of figurative language that compares two things or ideas using the word *like* or *as* (Lesson 1)

**social studies vocabulary** a word or phrase that has a particular meaning specific to social studies or history texts (Lesson 4)

**source** a publication that provides information (Lesson 8)

**spelling** the accepted arrangement of letters that make up a word (Lesson 8)

**stanza** a grouping of lines in a poem (Lesson 9)

**steps in a process** information presented in a sequence that must be followed in order to complete an action or arrive at a goal (Lesson 4)

**style** the words and sentences used in a text and how they are put together (Lesson 8)

**subject pronoun** a pronoun used as the subject in a sentence (Lesson 5)

**summarize** to restate the main points of a text (Lessons 3, 4, 7)

**supporting details** facts, statistics, explanations, data, and other evidence that help to convey the central idea of a text (Lessons 2, 4, 8, 10, 12)

**supporting reasons** statements that a writer makes to defend his or her opinion (Lesson 12); see *supporting details*

**technical text** a text that provides information about a technical subject (Lesson 7)

**text structure** how a text is organized, such as by sequence, cause and effect, or comparing and contrasting (Lessons 4, 7)

**theme** the central message of a text (Lessons 3, 6, 9)

**thesis** a statement that presents the main argument of a piece of writing, usually found in the introduction of the text (Lesson 10)

**time line** a graphic that shows sequence of events (Lessons 7, 8)

**tone** the author's attitude toward a topic (Lesson 3); how something is said (Lesson 8)

**topic** what a piece of writing is about (Lessons 2, 8)

**transition** a word or phrase that indicates the passage of time or order of events (Lessons 2, 8, 10, 12)

**vague pronoun** a pronoun with an unclear or unidentified antecedent (Lesson 10)

**word choice** the words or phrases selected by an author to convey his or her meaning (Lesson 3)

## Acknowledgments

**Picture Credits** 5–9, 12 Thinkstock.com; 8(b), 13 Wikimedia Commons; 17, 20, 41, 44 Thinkstock.com; 55 Wikimedia Commons; 56–59 (bkgrd) Thinkstock.com; 56 Library of Congress; 58, 62, 63(b) Wikimedia Commons; 63(t) Library of Congress; 67, 69, 91 Thinkstock.com; 92–95 Element, LLC; 105 Wikimedia Commons; 106–109, 117, 119, 120, 128(t) Thinkstock.com; 128(b) Wikimedia Commons; 145, 150–152, 155, 157–159 Thinkstock.com; 160, 162 U.S. Fish and Wildlife Service; 183–187, 195, 197 Thinkstock.com

**Illustrations** Cover Carl Wiens; 42–47 Peter Ferguson; 51–52 Steven Petruccio; 92–95 Lyle Miller; 98–102 Rich Longmore; 108–109, 113 Ivan Stalio; 147 Eric Freeberg; 190–192 Francesca D'Ottavi